IDEOLOGIES AND SOCIAL WORK

Subject Curriculum Series for Social Work Education

IDEOLOGIES AND SOCIAL WORK

Historical and Contemporary Analyses

MURLI DESAI

RAWAT PUBLICATIONS
Jaipur and New Delhi

ISBN 81-7033-736-4

Published by
Prem Rawat for ***Rawat Publications***
Satyam Apts., Sector 3, Jain Temple Road, Jawahar Nagar, Jaipur - 4 (India)
Phone: 0141 651748 / 657006 Fax: 0141 651748
E-mail : info@rawatbooks.com
Website: rawatbooks.com

Delhi Office
G-4, 4832/24, Ansari Road, Daryaganj, New Delhi 110 002
Phone: 011-3263290

Typeset by Rawat Computers, Jaipur
Printed at Chaman Enterprises, New Delhi

Dedicated to
Social Work students of the
Tata Institute of Social Sciences (1993-2002)

Contents

Foreword — P.D. Kulkarni 10
Prologue 12
List of Summary Charts 16

CONCEPTUAL FRAMEWORK AND CURRICULUM PLANNING 17
Conceptual Framework
Teacher/Learner Objectives
Structure and Content
Methodology of Social Work Education

CURRICULUM MODULES
1 WESTERN HISTORY OF IDEOLOGIES FOR SOCIAL CHANGE 44
Teacher/Learner Objectives
Ancient Period
Greek Ideologies
Medieval Period
Judeo-Christian Ideologies
Secular Humanism
Protestantism
Modern Period
Rationalism
Welfarism
Liberalism and Democracy
Utilitarianism and Social Darwinism
Socialism
Human Rights

2 WESTERN HISTORY OF IDEOLOGIES OF SOCIAL WORK PROFESSION 75
Teacher/Learner Objectives
Organised and Scientific Charity
Beginning of Social Work Education
Clinical Social Work
Ecological Social Work
Types, Levels, Roles and Process of Social Work Practice
Attributes of Professions
Professionalisation of Social Work

3 INDIAN HISTORY OF IDEOLOGIES FOR SOCIAL CHANGE 104
Teacher/Learner Objectives
Ancient Period
Vedic Ideology
Jainism and Buddhism
Spirituality
Medieval Period
Zoroastrianism in India
Islam in India
Mysticism of Bhakti and Sufi Movements
Sikhism
Modern Period
Christianity in India
Hindu Reform Movements
Dalit and Labour Movements
Gandhian Ideology and Sarvodaya Movement
Nationalism
Ideology of the Indian Constitution
Ideology of Voluntary Organisations

4 INDIAN HISTORY OF IDEOLOGIES OF SOCIAL WORK PROFESSION 135
Teacher/Learner Objectives
Beginning of Social Work Education
Professionalisation of Social Work

5 CONTEMPORARY IDEOLOGIES FOR SOCIAL CHANGE 151
Teacher/Learner Objectives
Neo-liberalism
Postmodernism
Feminism
Resurgence of the Civil Society
Multiculturalism
Ideologies of Sustainable and People-Centred Development
Ideologies of Action Groups and New Social Movements
Ideologies of Non-Government Organisations

6 CONTEMPORARY IDEOLOGIES OF SOCIAL WORK PROFESSION 180
Teacher/Learner Objectives
Ideologies that have Marginalised Vulnerable Groups
Limitations of professional Social Work
Contemporary Ideologies for Social Change and Professional Social Work
Contemporary Process of Systemic Marginalisation of Vulnerable Groups
Emerging Ideologies xf Professional Social Work and the Challenges Ahead

EPILOGUE: IMPLICATIONS FOR CONTEMPORARY SOCIAL WORK EDUCATION 202
The Contemporary Context and Objectives of Social Work Profession
Objectives of Social Work Education
Subject Framework for Social Work Education
Methodology of Social Work Education

References 213
Index 228

Foreword

This book on *Ideologies and Social Work* promises to be the first of a whole series of what are intended as sourcebooks for curriculum planning for social work education.

Having read this book in manuscript, I discovered that this is a very ambitious path breaker of massive dimensions. It is so rich and comprehensive in contents that it is bound to upgrade and sustain the quality of education currently being given in the 120 odd schools of social work in India. That this should have come 66 years after the introduction of professional social work education in India reflects on the pace and pattern of social work education. However it is heartening to note that this series of sourcebooks is being launched at the dawn of the 21st century just in time to respond effectively to the challenges of the new century.

Professional education in any profession cannot be "autonomous". Almost by definition, it must be relevant to the situational reality around it and must be practical enough to effectively tackle the problems on the ground. What is therefore needed is a central agency, which can review and foresee the changing reality and steer the educational programme accordingly. It is the Social Work Education and Practice Cell at the Tata Institute of Social Sciences, which has been doing this critical work quietly but steadfastly. Dr. Murli Desai who heads this cell has shown the vision and the grit to successfully complete this first foundational publication of the series. She has achieved just in a decade what few other professions or fewer other countries have done in much longer periods.

Personally, I have some different perspective on some of the assumptions and observations made in this book. But I notice that Dr. Desai has herself an open mind on the subject. She quotes Roche and others (1999) to say that "social work curriculum is a process of critical conversation", among all concerned.

I am confident that this series of sourcebooks will prove immensely valuable to teachers, students, practitioners and researchers, in social work in India and abroad.

P.D. Kulkarni
Formerly Social Work Educator and
United Nations Advisor, Social Development

Prologue

Development of resources for social work education such as subject curricula and methodology of social work education is one of the major activities of the Social Work Education and Practice Cell, that aims at strengthening of social work education in India. A Subject Curriculum Series for Social Work Education is, therefore, initiated with this book.

This book on *Ideologies and Social Work* is prepared as an outcome of preparation for teaching the course on the History and Philosophy of Social Work to first year students of MA in Social Work at the Tata Institute of Social Sciences (TISS), since 1993. It attempts to add to the much needed literature in the field as the last book on the subject was published by A.R. Wadia in 1961. It will be useful for the 125 institutions of social work education in India, each of which offers this subject. The Model Curriculum on Social Work Education by the University Grants Commission (2001) lists two subjects: Social Work History and Ideologies and Contemporary Ideologies for Social Work in the core domain of social work education.

This book uses the term 'ideologies' in the title instead of 'philosophy'. Philosophy is a form of inquiry or study of the mysteries of existence and reality through a process analysis, criticism, interpretation and speculation (Feibleman, 1986). Ideology resembles philosophy, but it is a system of thought based on related assumptions, beliefs and explanations that imply inevitability of choice, choice unsupported by reason, and its urgency (Hunt, 1978). It is the ideologies, rather than the philosophies, that seem to have influenced social change and, therefore, social work. It is the history of ideologies that helps us understand the roots of the contemporary reality, including the roots of the profession of social work. In social work, one uses the terms 'approaches' to convey differences in the forms of intervention. These approaches also can be understood better with reference to the ideologies that influence them.

The concepts of history, ideology and social work are organised in a conceptual framework, in order to analyse as well as make comparisons across social work approaches. The history of origin and development of an ideology or social work approach is first examined in its sociological/cultural/political/economic context. While linking different ideologies, the critique and implications of the previous ideology/approach are also examined, as these are often the context for a new ideology/approach to emerge. The construct of ideology of an approach comprises of the perception of people and of social problems, the ideals and the ethics, status of the benefactors and their motives for being benefactors, their goals for social change, their approach to social change/intervention, and their relation with the beneficiaries.

Besides the introductory chapter on conceptual framework and curriculum planning, the typescript is divided into six curriculum modules. These modules are arranged to undertake a critical inquiry into the Western history of ideologies before the Indian history of ideologies, as the former has influenced the latter since the modern age. Similarly, the history of ideologies of social change is examined before the history of ideologies of social work profession as the latter developed in the context of the former. The contemporary ideologies for social change and social work are then discussed in the context of globalisation. The methodology of education that is suggested aims at exploring and understanding one's own set of beliefs, based on one's socialisation.

A vast amount of relevant literature is available in the disciplines of sociology, political science, history, philosophy and social work, on each of these modules and on many of the topics within each module. It has been a mammoth task to identify the relevant matter and present it in a language that is succinct and digestible to students, at the risk of oversimplifying the matter. While carrying out this task, the overall purpose and context of social work education and the varied disciplinary backgrounds of social work students have been kept in mind. I must say that organising knowledge for teaching this subject has been a most gratifying experience for me. Understanding the history of ideologies for social change has helped me understand the roots of social problems of today, the limitations of the ideologies of professional social work to deal with them as well as directions for the profession in the contemporary times.

I take this opportunity to thank my co-teachers for this course, Ms. Jeroo Billimoria, Prof. Vimla Nadkarni and Mr. Parth Sarthi Mondal, for their suggestions and encouragement for this book. The course plan was reviewed in a small group as a part of the MA programme in social work at the Institute. While the book was being prepared, I presented several papers based on it at national and international seminars. The discussion that followed helped me to enrich the modules further. Most of all, every batch of students whom I taught, taught me how to teach the next batch better. I dedicate this compendium to these students. I immensely thank Prof. P.D. Kulkarni for writing a foreword to this book. Lastly, I would like to acknowledge the suggestions made by Prof. R.R. Singh,

Director, Tata Institute of Social Sciences for his suggestions to further enrich the typescript. I hope that departments of applied social sciences as well as schools of social work will find this book useful for reference for their curriculum planning and students will find it useful for studying the course.

Murli Desai
Professor and Head
Social Work Education and Practice Cell
Tata Institute of Social Sciences

List of Summary Charts

1 Classification of Ideologies for Social Change 43

2 Western Ideologies in their Historical and Societal Context and Implications 73

3 Influence of Western Modern Ideologies on Attributes of a Profession and Implications of Professionalisation of Social Work 102

4 Comparison of Professional Social Work with Social Movements 103

5 Indian Ideologies in their Historical and Societal Context and Implications 133

6 Influences on Ideologies of Professional Social Work in India 150

7 Understanding Neo-liberalism 176

8 Modernism versus Postmodernism and their Implications 177

9 Key Foci and Implications of Contemporary Ideologies 178

10 Historical Mode of Production and Systemic Marginalisation 199

11 Systemic Marginalisation of Vulnerable Groups 200

12 Prejudicing Ideologies and Marginalised Groups 201

Conceptual Framework and Curriculum Planning

This chapter starts with the conceptual framework to be used for a subject on history of ideologies for social change and social work, linking its major concepts. The teacher/learner objectives are drawn from this framework with reference to information, skills and attitude. The structure of the subject is divided into two two-credit hour parts to be offered in two semesters. The content of the subject is then presented in six modules. The relevant methodology of education for the subject is suggested in the areas of methods of teaching/learning, tools of teaching/learning and methods of assessment.

CONCEPTUAL FRAMEWORK

Social work practice is based on ideologies and it is impossible to understand the ideologies of the social work of today, without the knowledge of its roots in the historical ideologies of social work. Ideologies of social work, at any point of history, are influenced by the ideologies of social change of that time. As Katherine Kendall (2000) notes, social work, more than any other profession, is deeply rooted in the beliefs and social climate of the times in which it is practised. What seemed right in one period may appear wrong in another, she states.

The conceptual framework for a subject on history of ideologies for social change and social work may link the three constructs of history of social change, ideologies, and social work profession. The students need to examine this analysis with reference to the ideologies with which they are socialised.

History of Social Change

History is a discipline that studies the chronological record of events (as affecting a nation or people), based on a critical examination of source materials and usually presenting an explanation of their causes (*Encyclopaedia Britannica*, 2001). It is a study of the development of human society and its relationship with the present. Historical research emphasises the socio-cultural, political and economic context of events. Since about 1965, there has been some convergence between sociology and anthropology, on the one hand, and history, on the other. Historians have become interested in theories of long-term social change, while many sociologists and anthropologists increasingly turn towards history for the empirical testing and refinements of their theoretical viewpoints. Social change in the broadest sense is any change in social relations. In this sense, social change is an ever-present phenomenon in any society. In order to give the concept a more restricted meaning, it has been defined as change of the social structure (*Britannica.com*, 2000). However, the limitations of a historical study of social change are that sources are scarce, many activities and thoughts of ordinary people plus other useful data were never recorded and much that was written down has been lost or destroyed through the years. Thus, the past has to be reconstructed based on fragmented sources (*The World Book Encyclopedia*, 1988).

Periods of time form the chief divisions in the study of history. Historians divide Western history into three periods: ancient, medieval and modern. According to the Marxist theory of historical materialism, human beings make history, not in accordance with their arbitrary desires, but on the basis of the material conditions that take shape in the society at each stage of its development, which depends upon the mode of production (Berbeshkina, Yakovleva, and Zerkin, 1985). When the mode of production changes, the societal structure changes. According to the mode of production, a history may be divided into the hunting and gathering phase of the prehistorical period, agriculture and horticulture phase during the ancient and the medieval periods, the modern period of industrialisation and the post-industrialisation phase of the postmodern period.

In the prehistorical period, the productive means were hunting and gathering, for which people had to join efforts. Everything they procured was just enough to survive, which they shared among themselves equally. Such a primitive communal system may have existed for over tens of thousands of years (Berbeshkina and others, 1985). In the tribal system, natural resources were communally owned and property was more or less evenly distributed among the tribal members. However, the tribal chief, selected because of his hunting skills, had considerable political power and the shamans, or the medicine men lived off the surplus production of their followers. This system had a hierarchy, which was based on merits and could not be inherited (Grusky and Takata, 1992).

As surplus products developed, clans broke down into families. There was no longer any need for a joint economy and the family became an independent economic unit. People who farmed, no longer had to travel in search of food. They could thus build permanent settlements. In the agriculture and horticulture phase, need for labour led to the practice of marriage, slavery, and feudalism, institutionalising inequality. These practices were justified in terms of religious or quasi-religious ideologies such as natural and social inferiority (Grusky and Takata, 1992). When paternity was discovered through domestication of animals, and labour was needed for agriculture, by landed classes, patriliny through marriage was introduced. Collective labour was destroyed and women became economic producers for their male spouses and their families. It isolated women from one another through their articulation to men (Pandhe, 1989). Thus, marriage became a basic societal requirement for forming a family, implying that women's subordination to men was imperative for forming a family, in landed classes.

In the slavery system, those who were impoverished and became economically dependent on their kinsmen or fellow tribesfolk, through debts, were turned into slaves. Prisoners of war became another source of slaves. Slaves were property of their owners for whom they worked and got shelter, clothes and food, but no pay. Slaves could not marry, have a family, or own property (*The World Book Encyclopedia,* 1988). Slavery made it possible to build huge buildings and roads, in the ancient period. Contempt towards manual labour spread among exploiters who regarded it the fate of people of a lower sort (Berbeshkina and others, 1985).

Slavery gave way to feudalism, which became an important feature of the medieval period. The term feudalism is derived from the Latin word *feudum,* which means a piece of land which is granted in return of services (Kundra, 1997). In the feudal system, in return of protection, the serfs had to hand over their land and labour to their landlords and pay them their produce as levy. They had to necessarily send their paddy crop for husking to the rice mills owned by the landlords. Surplus produce had to be sold to the landlords alone. It was considered an offence if the serfs revolted against them (*Growth of Human Civilization*, 1993). Monarchies supported the slavery as well as the feudal systems, though they differed from one another in the degree to which power was centralised (Belov, 1986).

With the change in the predominant production process from agricultural to industrial, in the modern period, industries needed labour that was tied to the land. The political control of the landowning aristocracy and monarchies was challenged and foundations were laid for the modern nation-states (Ram, 1999). Individual merit was considered the determinant of status in the new class-stratification of the capitalist and the labour. However, this does not happen in practice, since the majority have already been deprived of the means of production and, therefore, also of the fruits of production (Kappen, 1994). The Industrial Revolution made European nationalism aggressive and expansionist, promoting international trade and colonisation of Asian and African countries. The pre-eminence of the nation-states grew as agencies of centralised social and political control, representing the interest of the capitalists against the people.

The hierarchy of the coloniser and the colonised was converted into the hierarchy of the 'developed' and the 'underdeveloped' after the colonies achieved independence. The Eurocentric paradigm of development of the colonisers was implemented within the ex-colonies, which led to a new hierarchy of the 'urban-organised' versus the 'rural-unorganised' (Sharma, 1998). Globalisation in the post-industrial period is neo-colonisation, placing a few global corporations above all the people of the world.

The subject of history of ideologies for social change and social work may examine the ideologies that have justified these unequal societal structures, ignored them, or tried to change them. The Western ideologies may be discussed before the Indian ones, as the former have influenced changes all over the world. The contemporary ideologies may be discussed in the context of globalisation.

Ideologies for Social Change

Philosophy is an academic discipline that seeks to understand the mysteries of existence and reality. It tries to discover the nature of truth and knowledge and to find what is of basic value and importance in life. It also examines the relationship between humanity and nature and between the individual and society. It is a form of interpretation and speculation. Philosophy is divided into five branches: metaphysics, epistemology, logic, ethics and aesthetics.

Ideology resembles philosophy, in that, it purports to answer the same substantive questions which the philosopher also confronts (*The World Book Encyclopedia*, 1988). However, according to Hunt (1978), the most important element in ideology is the inevitability of choice and its urgency. People who accept an ideology, usually reject all other systems concerned with the same content. It is a form of social or political philosophy in which practical elements are as prominent as theoretical ones. It is a system of ideas that aspires, both, to explain the world and to change it. (*Britannica.com*, 2000). According to Gore (1993), an ideology is a relatively comprehensive system of ideas, which gives legitimacy to an existing or proposed system of relationships, and correspondingly supports an action programme, to sustain or subvert the prevailing system. As this subject focuses on understanding social change, it prefers to study ideologies rather than philosophies.

Social change is generally influenced by religious and/or secular ideologies (see Summary Chart 1).

Religious Ideologies

Ideology originated in religious questions, that concerned the nature and purpose of life and death and the relationship of human to superhuman powers, or a divine creator. The subject matter of every religion comprises of the nature of 'God', cosmology or the science of creation, the nature of human beings, and the science of life after death. Every religion proclaims the existence of an immortal spirit, beyond body and mind and emphasises moral and ethical preparation for success in spiritual life. Most human beings are partisan with reference to religion; in the sense that they believe only in their own religion and do not accept the truth of another. A synthetic approach recognises that all religions are true and that diversity of religions is a law of nature (Swami Ghanananda, 1987).

The religions of the world fall into two well-defined groups: the eastern religions and the Judeo-Christian religions. The eastern religions, either owe their origin to India or are profoundly influenced by the Indian religious thought. The Vedic religion of India was followed by the non-Vedic Jainism and Buddhism, in the ancient period; and mysticism and Sikhism, in the medieval period. The Judeo-Christian religions owe their origin directly or indirectly to Judaism, an ancient religion of Israel. Judaism gave birth to Christianity and less directly to Islam, in the medieval period. In each case, there are religions originating in adjacent lands and ultimately assimilable by the two great religious streams; in the former case, Taoism and in the latter, Zoroastrianism (Zaehner, 1959). In India, all these religions have influenced each other and the society at different points of time. Religion provided the major source of ethics/morality/ideology for the society and for philanthropic work for a long time. Religions have justified social inequalities, on the one hand, and promoted altruism, for the disadvantaged, on the other.

Atheism and agnosticism, both, are forms of religious unbelief. Atheists say that they do not believe in the existence of God or Gods while agnostics say that they have inadequate knowledge to reach conclusions on the subject (Graves, 1995).

Secular Ideologies

Secular ideologies may be social, economic, political, and so on. The important Western secular ideologies that have brought far reaching changes all over the world are secular humanism, in the medieval period; rationalism, welfarism, liberalism, democracy, utilitarianism, Social Darwinism, socialism, and human rights, in the modern period; and the contemporary ideologies of neo- liberalism, feminism and postmodernism.

Ideologies and Social Movements

Religious and secular ideologies have influenced social movements that have brought about changes in social structures or created entirely new ones (Heberle, 1968). Gore (1993) observed that social movements have acted simultaneously at two levels: gaining legitimacy for a new value system and seeking reordering of relationships in one or more spheres of life in the light of the new values. As these movements disturb an existing pattern of exchange between groups, these are met with resistance. He further observed that movements end when they succeed in attaining their specific goals, or become part of larger movements, or cease to be relevant in a changed social context. The important social movements in India have been the Bhakti and Sufi movements, influenced by the ideology of mysticism in the medieval period; the Hindu reform movements influenced by the Western liberal ideology, and the Sarvodaya movement, led by the Gandhian philosophy, in the modern period; and the new social movements, influenced by several contemporary ideologies.

Social Work Profession

Professionalisation of social work to deal with social problems, is an outcome of the modern ideologies in the 20th century. Ripple (1969) defined the word profession to mean a public pronouncement or avowal of a belief or a promise. The promise is to attend in the most responsible, that is, the most knowledgeable way, the attainment of certain goals. According to Merton (1960), the following three social values are fused into the concept of a profession: (1) the value placed upon systematic knowledge and the intellect: knowing; (2) the value placed on technical skill and training capacity: doing; and (3) the value placed upon putting this conjoint knowledge and skill to work in the service of others: helping.

Different approaches have dominated professional social work, at different points of time in different places, such as charity, welfare, clinical, ecological and radical/progressive.

Conceptual Framework for Analysis of History of Ideologies and Social Work

The concepts of history, ideology and social work are organised in a conceptual framework, in order to analyse as well as make comparisons across social work approaches. The history of origin and development of an ideology or social work approach is first examined in its sociological/cultural/political/economic context. While linking different ideologies, the critique and implications of the previous ideology/approach are also examined, as these are often the context for a new ideology/approach to emerge. The construct ideology of an approach comprises of the perception of people and of social problems, the ideals and the ethics. For the construct of social work, the additional variables examined are, status of the benefactors and their motives for being benefactors, their goals for social change, their approach to social change/intervention, and their relation with the beneficiaries.

The conceptual framework to study history of ideology and social work thus comprises of the following components:

1. Historical context of origin and development of an ideology/approach to social change,
2. Perception of people and of social problems,
3. Ideals and ethics,
4. Status of the benefactors and their motives,
5. Rationale and goals for social change,
6. Approach to social change/intervention and relation of benefactors with the beneficiaries, and
7. Historical/contemporary critique and implications.

Ideology of Social Work Students

Every person has an ideology without knowing it, which one holds so deeply that one thinks, feels and acts in the world by means of it, without even being aware of its existence (Feibleman, 1986). One's ideology includes one's perception of people and reasons for social problems, one's values and ethics, and one's goal and approach to social change, influenced by one's socialisation.

According to Goldstein (1973), besides one's ideology, every person has sentient characteristics that are affective and responsive attributes which determine the way he or she perceives, feels, relates and responds to his or her social reality; in short, his or her capacity for awareness. Two orders of sentient characteristics are, the responsive and the interpersonal. The responsive characteristics are those internal reactions that add to knowing and understanding, which include sensitivity, empathy and intuition. The interpersonal characteristics are the capabilities for acceptance and commitment in relationship with others.

The ideological elements of moral, ethical and metaphysical factors are for the most part intrinsic to every person and comprise the basic attitudes, beliefs and values -- the "self". These are usually unstructured, unquestioned and unarticulated. It is necessary that a social work student bring one's ideology and that of the profession into cognition. This revelation will lead itself to conscious deliberation and then resolution (Goldstein, 1973).

TEACHER/LEARNER OBJECTIVES

Social work education requires knowledge-as-action, knowledge that is contextualised culturally and historically and is shaped by the interaction between students and teachers. It is, therefore, necessary to treat social work curriculum as a process of critical conversation (Roche, Dewees, Trailweaver, Alexander, Cuddy and Handy, 1999). This course aims at introducing the students to a critical inquiry into the history of ideologies of social change and professional social work. The specific teacher/learner objectives of the course are related to the following information, skill and attitude areas:

Information Objectives

Students gain information about the Western and Indian religious ideologies and ideologies for social change with reference to the following aspects in order to understand the historical roots of social problems, of social work profession and of the contemporary ideologies:

- Historical context of origin and development of an ideology/approach to social change,
- Perception of people and of social problems,
- Ideals and ethics,
- Status of the benefactors and their motives,
- Rationale and goals for social change,

- Approach to social change/intervention and relation of benefactors with the beneficiaries, and
- Historical/contemporary critique/implications.

Students may also gain knowledge about ideologies of professional social work approaches, linked to ideologies for social change, and their limitations, and arrive at future directions.

Skill Objectives

Students develop the following skills of critical inquiry into:

- understanding of contemporary social reality in its historical context, and
- understanding of self as part of one's environment.

Attitude Objectives

Students explore their own assumptions, ideals, values and experiences about people and their problems in order to do the following:

- be sensitive to systemic marginalisation of vulnerable groups, and
- examine the emerging value framework and ethical responsibilities of social work.

Objectives by Modules

To meet the above objectives the subject is planned in the following modules:

Module 1: Western History of Ideologies for Social Change

Module 2: Western History of Ideologies of Social Work Profession

Module 3: Indian History of Ideologies for Social Change

Module 4: Indian History of Ideologies of Social Work Profession

Module 5: Contemporary Ideologies for Social Change

Module 6: Contemporary Ideologies of Social Work Profession

The Western history of ideologies is analysed before the Indian history of ideologies, as the former has influenced the latter since the modern age. Similarly, the history of ideologies of social change is examined before the history of ideologies of social work profession as the latter developed in the context of the former. The contemporary ideologies for social change and social work are then discussed in the context of globalisation.

The module on 'Western History of Ideologies for Social Change' may examine how secular humanism and Protestantism revived the importance of human beings, and promoted individualism and work ethics, in the religion-dominated feudal society of the Western world, by the end of the medieval period; analyse the way rationalism, welfarism, liberalism, and democracy led to emergence of science, nation-states and the middle class in the West, in the beginning of the modern period; study how utilitarianism and Social Darwinism promoted international trade, justified colonisation, leading to Industrial Revolution, and established the capitalistic paradigm of development all over the world, dividing it into the First World and the Third World; analyse the role played by socialism to counter the uncontrolled growth of liberalistic ideologies and in the emergence of the Second World; and examine the dynamics of the United Nations human rights instruments, after the Second World War, in further promoting individualism and liberalism.

The module on 'Western History of Ideologies of Social Work Profession' may help examine how the Western modern ideologies have led to requirements of a profession, such as social work, in terms of secularisation of help and importance of scientific knowledge, formal education and specialisations;

understand the liberalistic context of predominance of the clinical approach in social work profession in the US and its implications for support from the capitalists and the state; understand the influence of the systems theory on social work and the emergent ecological social work approach; examine the types, levels, roles and process of social work practice; and study the professionalisation of the normative and the cognitive attributes of social work in the US and its implications for the profession, becoming an end in itself.

The module on 'Indian History of Ideologies for Social Change' may examine the plurality of religious ideologies, that have influenced social change in India, the development of the Vedic and non-Vedic ideologies in the context of the Aryan invasion and the emergence of the caste system in India, in the ancient period; analyse the influence of Islam in India, during the Turk and Moghul rule and the emergence of mysticism of Bhakti and Sufi movements and Sikhism, in the medieval period; study the influence of Christianity and modern ideologies in India, during the British rule, and the emergence of Hindu reform movements and Dalit movements; understand the Gandhian ideology and Sarvoday movement and nationalism, during the freedom movement of India; and analyse the ideology of the Indian Constitution as influenced by the United Nations' Universal Declaration of Human Rights and Indian nationalism and the role of voluntary organisations, after independence.

The module on 'Indian History of Ideologies of Social Work Profession' may analyse the influence of the Western ideology of professional social work and the Indian ideologies for social change on ideologies of social work profession in India and examine the professionalisation of the normative and the cognitive attributes of social work in India.

The module on 'Contemporary Ideologies for Social Change' may examine the transition from liberalism to the hegemonic ideology of neo-liberalism, leading to globalisation in the contemporary times; compare the emerging ideology of postmodernism with that of modernism; analyse the ideologies that are trying to counter neo-liberalism, namely, second wave feminism, resurgence of the civil society, multiculturalism and sustainable and people-centred development; and understand the ideologies and roles played by action groups, new social movements and non-government organisations.

The module on 'Contemporary Ideologies of Social Work Profession' may summarise the ideologies for social change that have lead to marginalisation of vulnerable groups and their problems and understand that the same ideologies have led to professionalisation of social work, so the profession has limitations in dealing with these problems; summarise the contemporary ideologies that are trying to counter the marginalising ideologies and examine their linkages to professional social work; analyse the contemporary process of systemic marginalisation of vulnerable groups through prejudicing ideologies, linked to access to resources and power, and reinforced by social systems; and examine the emerging ideologies of social work profession and the challenges in realising their ideals.

STRUCTURE AND CONTENT

Structure

The subject is suggested to be offered for two semesters in two parts, one dealing with the 'History of Ideologies of Social Change and Social Work' (30 hours) and the other with 'Contemporary Ideologies of Social Change and Social Work' (30 hours). Each of the two parts may first examine the Western history of ideologies first, then the Indian history of ideologies. This structure is elaborated as follows:

SEMESTER 1	
Part 1: History of Ideologies for Social Change and Social Work	30 hours
Introduction to the Course and Part 1	2 hours
Module 1: Western History of Ideologies for Social Change	6 hours
Module 2: Western History of Ideologies of Social Work Profession	6 hours
Module 3: Indian History of Ideologies for Social Change	6 hours
Module 4: Indian History of Ideologies of Social Work Profession	6 hours
Workshop	2 hours
Summary and Evaluation of Part 1	2 hours
SEMESTER 2	
Part 2: Contemporary Ideologies for Social Change and Social Work	30 hours
Introduction to Part 2	2 hours
Module 5: Contemporary Ideologies for Social Change	14 hours
Module 6: Contemporary Ideologies of Social Work Profession	10 hours
Workshop	2 hours
Summary of Part 2 of the Course and Course Evaluation	2 hours

The content of each Module is suggested as follows:

Module 1: Western History of Ideologies for Social Change

- Ancient Period:
  Greek ideologies

- Medieval Period:
  Judeo-Christian ideologies
  Secular humanism
  Protestantism
- Modern Period:
  Rationalism
  Welfarism
  Liberalism and democracy
  Utilitarianism and Social Darwinism
  Socialism and human rights

Module 2: Western History of Ideologies of Social Work Profession

- Organised and scientific charity
- Beginning of social work education
- Clinical social work
- Ecological social work
- Types, levels, roles and process of social work practice
- Attributes of a profession
- Professionalisation of social work

Module 3: Indian History of Ideologies for Social Change

- Ancient Period:
  Vedic ideologies
  Jainism and Buddhism
  Spirituality
- Medieval Period:
  Zoroastrianism in India
  Islam in India
  Mysticism of Bhakti and Sufi movements
  Sikhism

- Modern Period:
  Christianity in India
  Hindu reform movements
  Dalit and labour movements
  Gandhian ideology and Sarvoday movement
  Nationalism
  Ideology of the Indian Constitution
  Ideology of voluntary organisations

Module 4: Indian History of Ideologies of Social Work Profession

- Beginning of social work education
- Professionalisation of social work

Module 5: Contemporary Ideologies for Social Change

- Neo-liberalism
- Postmodernism
- Feminism
- Resurgence of the civil society
- Multiculturalism
- Ideologies of sustainable and people-centred development
- Ideologies of action groups and social movements
- Ideologies of non-government organisations

Module 6: Contemporary Ideologies of Social Work Profession

- Summary of ideologies that have marginalised vulnerable groups and limitations of professional social work
- Summary of contemporary ideologies for social change and professional social work

- Contemporary process of systemic marginalisation of vulnerable groups
- Emerging ideologies of professional social work and challenges ahead.

METHODOLOGY OF SOCIAL WORK EDUCATION

Methodology of social work education is as important to the learning process, as methodology in social work practice is, to the problem solving process. In order for the teacher-learner transaction to give the same dynamics to training as the worker-client transaction gives to practice, the educator should be a facilitator of learning rather than merely a transmitter of knowledge. The participation model of education is, therefore, more appropriate for social work education (Hokenstad and Rigby, 1977).

In social work education, the instructor is not the pre-eminent possessor of knowledge. Learners also bring their own interpretative powers to life experiences. Both are co-sharers in the creation of what is known. When no particular interpretation deserves to have a privileged status, then the intellectual skill of critique is essential. Students must learn how to approach, whatever content is presented, with means for critically assessing its virtues and shortcomings. To prepare students as reflective practitioners there is a need for expanded ways for them to appreciate their own wisdom and creativity (Weick, 1994).

The methodology of education should first plan to recognise the students' current knowledge level as valuable, and it should be brought to the fore through their participation. Knowledge and its analysis may then be imparted to them. Self-learning experiences should be planned to facilitate reflection and comprehension. Evaluation of the new knowledge should be encouraged to relate it to the current knowledge. The synthesis of the two will lead to application (Percival and Ellington, 1984).

Methods of Teaching/Learning

The course may use a combination of the following methods for teaching/learning:

- Lectures and discussion
- Inviting guest speakers/practitioners and discussion
- Experiential exercises and discussion
- Workshops
  - — Use of newspaper clippings, audio-visual aids and case studies
  - — Small group discussions
  - — Group assignments and presentations.

Workshop Tools

The following are some workshop tools that can be used for the subject:

Understanding of Social Work and Self

In the beginning of the course, a questionnaire with the following questions may be administered, and then the responses received may be discussed in class:

- What is social work?
- Why are there social problems?
- What do you think a social worker does about social problems?
- Is training required for social work?
- Why have you joined an education programme in social work?

- What qualities do you think you have, to be a social worker?
- How would you like to see yourself five years hence?

Role Play for Ideologies of Social Work Approaches

In order to learn the ideologies of different social work approaches, the teacher may involve the students in a role play as follows. Ask six students to volunteer to carry out the roles of no social work approach and five different social work approaches: charity, institutional and non-institutional welfare, clinical social work, and progressive social work. The following procedure may then be used:

1. Ask the class to behave as though they are people of a village who do not have ball pens. Ask the volunteers to behave as though they have ball pens and are visiting the village with different approaches. Give a brief script to each of them.
2. Start with the role play of the visitor who does not use any social work approach. Demonstrate the rationalisation of having ball pens, based on personal merits or inheritance, and indifference to the ball pen-have-nots.
3. The second visitor uses the charity approach to help the ball pen-have-nots. This person will give a ball pen each to some of the ball pen-have-nots. He/She will not have enough ball pens for all. He/She will then move away. Ask the ball pen-have-nots how they felt. Ask the charity giver how he/she felt. Emphasise the direct, impersonal and condescending approach in charity, which generally has the motive of religious merits, and cannot meet the needs of all the have-nots.
4. The next visitor demonstrates the institutional welfare approach. According to the script, this volunteer will announce an institution for the pen-have-nots. Some of the

ball pen-have-nots will be asked to get up from their chairs and gather in a corner, symbolising an institution. There are rules about who can be taken in, when and for how long. The literate and the illiterate are separated. Once they are in, they will be told not to leave the institution. Then give them writing services, that are of poor quality and inadequate. Ask the ball pen-have-nots how they felt. Ask the volunteer how he/she felt. Emphasise segregation through institutionalisation due to intolerance, separating the problem from its source, and controlling their mobility.

5. The volunteer using the non-institutional welfare approach sits on the chair and table on the dais as an agency. He/She will announce that it runs a government scheme, which provides ball pens, repairing ball pens and running a writing service centre for those who do not have ball pens. There are rules about who can come, when, for how long, and so on. Ask the pen-have-nots how they felt. Ask the volunteer how he/she felt. Emphasise that agency orientation has restraining rules that can make it an end in itself. It does not necessarily have the need orientation and the most needy may not even come to know about it.
6. The next visitor uses the clinical social work approach. He/She will also sit on the chair and table on the dais. He/She will announce oneself as a counsellor. When a ball pen-have-not comes to him/her, he/she will take his/her family history regarding ball pens, gives psychological tests and provides treatment to improve the client's psycho-social attitude to ball pens, and mechanisms to cope without them. Ask the pen-have-nots how they felt. Ask the volunteer how he/she felt. Emphasise that this approach does not recognise the environmental sources for people not having ball pens and, therefore, does not deal with them.

7. The last visitor uses the progressive social work approach. He/She will go to the pen-have-nots and talk to them about how they do not have ball pens because they are marginalised by the pen market and by the policies of the state, which supports the market. He/She will explain to them that they have a human right to have writing instruments, but they need not have ball pens. Ball pens are not eco-friendly. They can choose to use pencils, *kalams*, fountain pens or make ball pens themselves. They can do so, if they are together. Ask the pen-have-nots how they felt. Ask the volunteer how he/she felt. Emphasise that the pen-have-nots may be initially impatient to have ball pens but develop a new awareness about them and their needs for them, which is useful to solve the problem of not having ball pens.
8. Discuss that these approaches have evolved in their historical context and they all are needed and exist today.

Use of Newspaper Clippings, Audio-Visual Aids and Case Studies

The teacher may introduce a newspaper clipping/audio-visual aid/a case study with reference to a marginalised group and ask the students to answer the following questions:

1. Which person/group in this article is marginalised and which group do they represent at the macro level?
2. What are the reasons for their marginalisation? Which resources does this group not have control over that keeps them marginalised?
3. What does the Indian Constitution provide for this group in terms of Fundamental Rights and Directive Principles?
4. Which person/group in this article has power? Which group does it represent at the macro level? What are the resources that this group has control over, which keeps them in power?

5. Which systems perpetuate the marginalisation?
6. What prejudicing ideologies justify the unequal access to resources?

Methods of Assessment

The course could use a combination of assignments and examination for assessment of the students.

Assignment on Ideology of Self

An assignment on ideology of self may be given with the following questions:

1. What are your strong values and beliefs and what are the factors that have influenced and are influencing these?
2. Review a book on the ideology of the person that has influenced your values and beliefs strongly, using the following format:
   (a) Rationale for selection of the book
   (b) Introduction to the author
   (c) Introduction to the historical background of the book/person
   (d) Understanding of people and social problems
   (e) Philosophy, ideology, values and ethics
   (f) Intervention with people and/or social problems
   (g) Relevance to the current situation
   (h) Relevance to social work
   (i) Influence on one's values and beliefs

Assignment on Ideology of Others

The above assignment may be given with reference to values and beliefs of a classmate.

Assignment on Social Sensitivity

An assignment on social sensitivity may be given with the following questions:

1. What assumptions do others have about you because of your sex and your family's religion, caste/tribe, regional and class background? Have these assumptions affected your or your family's access to different resources? How have these factors influenced your self identity?
2. What assumptions have you developed about people with sex, religion, caste/tribe, regional background, class, age and abilities other than yours? What are the bases/sources for these assumptions?
3. Have you experienced power over others or powerlessness with reference to others because of your sex, religion, caste/tribe, regional background, class, age and abilities ?
4. How have these assumptions and experiences affected your relationship with people with reference to the following?
   (a) Awareness of individuality and ability to avoid stereotypes
   (b) Acceptance of differences in others
   (c) Sensitivity to feelings and needs of others.

Examination

Following are some relevant questions for examination:

1. Compare the ideologies of historical materialism with Social Darwinism to explain social change.
2. Compare religious and secular ideologies.
3. Explain how the Western ideologies influenced the rest of the world.
4. Compare the ideologies of liberalism and socialism and their influence on human rights and feminism.

5. Explain how the Western modern ideologies have influenced professionalisation of social work and its implications.
6. Compare the role of professional social work with that of social movements for social change.
7. Compare the ideologies of clinical and ecological social work.
8. Compare the ideologies for social change developed in the West and those in India.
9. Compare the social movements in India during the Muslim rule, British rule and after independence.
10. Compare professionalisation of social work in the US and in India.
11. Compare modern and postmodern ideologies.
12. Discuss the ideologies of professional social work in India with reference to its sources in modern ideologies, Indian ideologies and contemporary ideologies for social change.
13. Analyse the emerging ideologies of social work with reference to the contemporary ideologies for social change.
14. Examine the challenges posed by the emerging ideologies of social work profession and identify your role in it.

Summary Chart 1

Classification of Ideologies for Social Change

	Religious Ideologies	*Secular Ideologies*
Period of origin	Ancient and medieval	Medieval and modern
Subject matter	Faith with reference to nature, purpose of life and death and relationship of human to superhuman powers	A system of thought based on related assumptions, beliefs and explanations that legitimate a societal structure
Types	Eastern religions, Judeo-Christian religions	Social, political, economic

Module 1

Western History of Ideologies for Social Change

TEACHER/LEARNER OBJECTIVES

The module on 'Western History of Ideologies for Social Change' may have the following teacher/learner objectives:

1. Understand how secular humanism and Protestantism revived the importance of human beings, and promoted individualism and work ethics in the religion-dominated feudal society of the Western world, by the end of the medieval period.
2. Examine the way rationalism, welfarism, liberalism, and democracy led to emergence of science, nation-states and the middle class in the West in the beginning of the modern period.
3. Study how utilitarianism and Social Darwinism promoted international trade, justified colonisation, leading to

Industrial Revolution, and established the capitalistic paradigm of development in most parts of the world, dividing it into the First World and the Third World.

4. Analyse the role played by socialism to counter the uncontrolled growth of liberalistic ideologies and in the emergence of the Second World.
5. Examine the dynamics of the United Nations human rights instruments after the Second World War, in further promoting individualism and liberalism.

ANCIENT PERIOD

Greek Ideologies

Historical Context of Origin and Development

By the 5th century BC, of the ancient period, Greece was a collection of independent city-states. They had direct democracy, with every man voting on every important issue. However, slaves and women could not participate in it.

Ideals, Rationale and Goals for Social Change

For the Greeks, in the ancient period, nature was central, and all-inclusive, human beings second and God third. Both, human beings and God were considered part of nature, but human beings were more important than God. The famous Greek philosophers of this period were Socrates, Plato and Aristotle. According to Socrates, success could never be more than a short-term affair unless it was founded on logical truth and moral right. Socrates wrote nothing; it is through the writings of his student Plato that we know about him (Feibleman, 1986).

Plato elaborated Socrates' pursuit of truth. He distinguished between a world of material objects in space and time, corresponding to the report of our senses, and a world of abstract ideas, corresponding to our thoughts. He recommended the pleasures of abstract ideas as eternal as against the short-lived pleasures of the sensual type. In his book *Republic*, he outlined the ideal state, through which he sought to discover justice. He preferred statesmen rather than politicians to rule the state as ruling required special knowledge and ideology (Feibleman, 1986).

Aristotle was Plato's student who gave Plato's ideas a more practical turn. His dreaming was less imaginative but his observations were sharper than those of Plato. He thought that there was only one external world, but it was a material world which, at the same time, contained the ideas (Feibleman, 1986).

Implications

As Rome gained ascendancy, during 200 BC, Greece became a small and unimportant part of the Roman Empire. The decline of the political importance of Greece led to the decline of the Greek ideology. However, the Romans spread the Greek literature, paintings, sculpture, theatre and architecture more widely than the Greeks themselves had done (*The World Book Encyclopedia,* 1988).

MEDIEVAL PERIOD

Judeo-Christian Ideologies

Historical Context of Origin and Development

Judaism can be dated to about 1700 BC, much before the Greek philosophers lived. Christianity was originally a social movement in Judaism (Marshall, 1994). What Jesus Christ wanted was to reform Judaism and not to replace it. He nowhere refers to himself as the founder of Christianity.

Christianity emerged as a separate religion only when it had been rejected by the majority of the Jews. When Romans occupied Israel, they were exposed to Christianity. Paul, a Roman citizen, was a major initiator of the spread of Christianity, which was adopted as the official religion of the Roman Empire. After the fall of the Western Roman Empire, around 400 AD, Europe was divided into a number of regional powers. Christianity replaced it as the unifying force in Western Europe, with the Pope exercising religious as well as political authority. This change marks the beginning of the medieval period. During this time, up to the 1600s, Western ideology developed more as a part of Christian theology (*The World Book Encyclopedia,* 1988).

The growth of feudalism was an important feature of the medieval period. The weak kings had lost control over the governance and had to rely on the nobles for the defence of the empire as they had strong and loyal armies of knights. The nobles obtained land from the kings in return of support in defence. The nobles became stronger than the kings also because the farmers also needed their protection. The farmers, therefore, willingly handed over their lands and labour to the nobles in the vicinity and secured the right to till their own lands as tenants. Gradually the feudal lords usurped the lands of these tenants and made them serfs (*Growth of Human Civilization*, 1993).

Many feudal lords gave lands to the church in return for services performed by the clergy. The clergy also lived like the feudal lords. The Roman Catholic Church not only considered the feudal system a result of divine ordinance, it also became the largest landholder during this time. At first the feudal lords controlled the church, but gradually the church dominated them with the power of threat of excommunication (*The World Book Encyclopedia,* 1988).

Perception of People and Social Problems

According to Judaism, Adam and Eve committed the 'original sin' when they violated the commandment of God by eating the forbidden fruit. Their descendants forever were to inherit the guilt, needing redemption (McCasland, Cairns and Yu, 1969). Christians believe that salvation from punishment has been made possible by God's mercy in sending a saviour – Jesus Christ -- to atone for these sins (Marshall, 1994). Christianity also teaches that after Jesus' earthly life, God's presence remained on earth in the form of the Holy Spirit or Holy Ghost. The belief that in one God there are three persons -- the Father, the Son and the Holy Spirit – is known as the doctrine of the Trinity (*The World Book Encyclopedia*, 1988).

Ideals, Rationale and Goals for Social Change

The cornerstone of Judaism is the Hebrew Bible, or the Old Testament. According to the interpretation of Judaism in the medieval period, the following 13 articles of faith comprise its essential dogmas: The existence of God, the creator of all things; His absolute unity; His incorporeality; His eternity; the obligation to serve and worship Him alone; the existence of prophecy; the superiority of the prophecy of Moses above all others; the Torah as God's revelation to Moses; the immutability of the Torah; God's omniscience and foreknowledge; reward and punishment according to one's deeds; the coming of the Messiah; and the resurrection of the dead (Zwi Werblowsky, 1959).

Christianity retained the importance of the Hebrew Bible and the essentials of the Jewish ideology as fundamental to its own faith. Jesus Christ used the Ten Commandments as the basis for his moral and ethical teachings. He indicated that love is the essential element of religion, in the form of love for God and love for neighbours. This life is considered the only chance to implement the will of God, which is to be as kind as Him. The Roman Catholic Church is the common name of the worldwide organisation of Christians who recognise the authority of the Pope and give their allegiance to him. The Catholic belief is that God has established the church, administered by its priests, whose responsibility is to offer the sacraments through which His divine grace is made available to people (McCasland and others, 1969).

Approach to Social Change

In Judaism, the highest form of charity is to help the poor rehabilitate themselves by lending them money, taking them into partnership or employing them. The Jews levied a tithe (tax) for the poor. Christianity prescribes that all believers must offer 10 per cent of their income as a measure of gratitude to God (Samuel, 1999). Churches use this income to maintain hospitals, schools, inns for travellers and other social services, for the people they serve.

Implications

The Judeo-Christian religions have comprised the dominant religious force in the development of the Western culture. The Roman Catholic Church had a major impact on the Western culture especially through the educational function of monasteries (Marshall, 1994). The power of the Pope was believed to be divine and final for social as well as political matters. This interference by the church led to conflict between the European rulers and the Pope (*Growth of Human Civilization*, 1993). Some people in mission lands resented foreign missionary activity because they persuaded people to accept foreign rule and insensitively imposed Western traditions and social values on native cultures (*The World Book Encyclopedia*, 1988).

Secular Humanism

Historical Context of Origin

During the 12th and the 13th centuries, trade increased and the barter economy was replaced by money economy. The new class of traders and merchants sided with the kings and the influence of the feudal nobles started declining. The new class needed the services of managers and clerks. These people were called the middle class, as they were neither feudal lords nor farmers. This middle class was educated and instrumental in laying the foundation of the Renaissance (*Growth of Human Civilization*, 1993).

The cultural movement of Renaissance overlapped with the end of the Middle Ages and formed a transition between medieval and modern ideology. The Renaissance movement began in Italy during the early 1300s. It spread to the rest of Western Europe in the late 1400s and ended about 1600. During this period, emphasis on science and humanism led to changes in the aims and techniques of philosophic inquiry, freeing ideology from its ties to medieval theology. Secular humanism formed the intellectual core of the Renaissance.

Perception of People and Social Problems

Scholars and artists of the late medieval period rediscovered the ancient humanistic works of the scholars and artists of ancient Greece and Rome and became more concerned with understanding people and the world, instead of the Christian religion (*The World Book Encyclopedia*, 1988). Humanism reclaimed dignity and a central position for the human being (Puledda, 1998).

Ideals, Rationale and Goals for Social Change

Secular humanism liberated humanity from religion. It questioned the absolute hegemony of the church in defining social life and life in the civil society. It replaced religion as the organising principle of modern state (Muricken, 1998). According to Sharma (1980), comprehensive humanism understands the totality of human nature and recognises human beings as the author of ethical, political and social judgements. It neither creates a fear-complex in human beings, as the dogmatism and excesses of orthodox religions have done, nor overemphasises the successes of science as the basis for its claim to absolute truth. It contends that moral obligations are to be discharged voluntarily by every person (Sharma, 1980).

The "Humanist Manifesto" of 1933, issued by a group of 34 persons, including John Dewey, stated that humanists hold an "organic view of life", reject the "traditional dualism of mind and body" and believe that "man is a part of nature and that he has emerged as the result of a continuous process" (Sharma, 1980).

Critique and Implications

The Western tradition of humanism became the ethical basis for civil society in the modern era (Puledda, 1998). Humanism led to secularism in politics, which led to separation of religion from politics. According to Ikeda (1998), humanity liberated from religion, found itself trapped by its own egotism. It has now come to be ordered by the dictates of desire and its gratification.

Protestantism

Historical Context of Origin and Development

With the influence of the Renaissance, the unrestrained authority of the church and its unscientific attitude began to be challenged. In the 16th century, corruption within the Catholic Church sparked off a religious movement called the

Reformation. It led to several Protestant groups, which set up new churches (*World History*, 1996).

Ideals, Rationale and Goals for Social Change

The reformers/Protestants rejected the authority of the Roman Catholic Church and turned to the Bible, instead, as their source of authority. The Bible was translated into English at this time. They stressed the importance of faith and rejected the emphasis that Roman Catholics place on good works. They believed that people were incapable of saving themselves because of their sins, and they receive salvation by having faith in God's grace, which comes to them through Christ (*The World Book Encyclopedia*, 1988).

According to Martin Luther, the leading reformer, work of any kind was service to God, and he endowed work with religious dignity by defining it as a vocation or a calling. In his view, people serve God best by doing most perfectly the work of their own vocation. Conversely, people who do not work, or will not work to the full extent of their ability, are sinners (Macarov, 1995). The concept of calling of ascetic Protestantism resulted in rationalisation of conduct within this world, for the sake of the world beyond. As human beings were considered only trustees of the goods which had come to them through God's grace, the greater the possessions, the heavier the feeling of responsibility for them, for holding them undiminished for the glory of God and increasing them by restless effort. This worldly Protestant asceticism had the psychological effect of freeing the acquisition of goods from the inhibitions of traditionalistic ethics. It favoured the development of a rational bourgeois life (Weber, 1958).

Critique and Implications

Protestantism provided legitimation to individualism, freedom (Feibleman, 1986) and the profit motive that contributed to the development of the values and personality traits that characterise the spirit of capitalism in the Western world (Weber, 1958). According to Max Weber (1958), the pursuit of wealth, stripped of its religious and ethical meaning, tended to become associated with purely mundane passions, with its inexorable power over the lives of human beings.

MODERN PERIOD

Rationalism

Historical Context of Origin

Rationalism is a philosophic outlook that arose in the 1600s, launching off the modern era. It ushered in an Age of Reason or Enlightenment for humankind, as opposed to what were now increasingly viewed as the superstitious and ignorant 'Dark Ages'. The Enlightenment project is supposed to have lasted until the late 1700s.

Ideals, Rationale and Goals for Social Change

The Enlightenment project was characterised by the gradual shift away from religious sensibilities to scientific objectivity. Reasoning replaced religion as the source of knowledge. The basic idea of rationalism is that reason is superior to experience as a source of knowledge and the validity of sense perception must be proved from more certain principles (*The World Book Encyclopedia*, 1988).

The 17th century philosophers in Europe emphasised the division between mind and matter. Philosophers focussed on the mind and left the inquiry about matter to science. Values were separated from facts, and ever since then we have tended to believe that scientific facts are independent of what we do and are, therefore, independent of our values (Capra, 1996).

Critique and Implications

As the 19th century closed, modern science was firmly embedded as the exemplar for discovering 'truth', and 'truth' (often described as reality) was equated only with the observable and measurable. Scientific humanism rejects every method of inquiry other than scientific (Geiger, 1947). Sharma (1980) observed that scientific humanists seem to be overwhelmed by its achievements in the same manner as ideology was overwhelmed by religion in the medieval period. Western science had assumed a God-like supremacy which was to endure throughout most of the 20th century (Ramsay, 1999).

Welfarism

Historical Context of Origin and Development

England was leading among the Protestant countries, in formulating non-sectarian laws to deal with the poor. In 1349, the Statute of Labourers required people to work. Begging and alms-giving were outlawed except for the "worthy" poor. During the time of the Reformation, in 1536, the Henrican Poor Law acknowledged that the state rather than the church or volunteers must play some role in caring for the poor. In 1572, a national tax, called the Parish Poor Rate, was levied to cover its costs (Barker, 1987).

During the 1600s, when science had begun to replace religion as the source of ultimate authority, scientists criticised that direct and religious charity was indiscriminate and not scientific. In response to this critique, England enacted the Elizabethan Poor Law in 1601. In the US, the Poor Law was implemented in 1642. In the 18th century, family-based outdoor relief (today also known as non-institutional services) was introduced (Barker, 1987).

Perception of People and Social Problems

The Elizabethan Poor Law provided for helpless people whose needs were large and likely to be prolonged – orphans, the handicapped, the chronically ill and the feeble aged (Leiby, 1987). It emphasised the difference between the "worthy" poor, who were impotent and the "unworthy" poor who were able-bodied. Both were considered responsible for their poverty. They were perceived as sources of political trouble, failures of the system, and those who only procreate but cannot maintain their children (Rao, 1994). Drawing from the Protestant work ethics, those who did not work were accused of sinfulness or immorality. This sharpened the distinction between the deserving and the undeserving poor (Macarov, 1995).

Benefactors and their Motives

The state represented the interests of the powerful and landed class. For the state, the public interest was what maintained the system of economic and social relations that the landed aristocracy was used to and benefitted from, and that advanced the control of the government (Reid, 1995). The government also had the motive of giving prominence to the state above the church. Far from being designed to provide a modicum of social security, poor relief was conceived of as a police measure. By preventing the despair of starvation, among the roving bands of beggars, it was expected to diminish the potential danger of desperate action and the ensuing disturbance to society (Macarov, 1995). Later, the liberalists urged the governments to allow free trade and provide social benefits for heavy losers, in the form of such consolations as unemployment insurance, old age pensions and so on, to prevent them from revolting (Boguslaw, 1992).

Approach to Intervention

The Elizabethan Poor Law defined the duty of the parish to relieve the poor, established overseers to perform it, and gave them power to raise funds and administer relief. This relief was the last resort when the ordinary informal help of family, neighbours and friends was not available or sufficient (Leiby, 1987). The able-bodied poor were forced to work in the workhouses and the impotent poor were placed in the alms-houses. The residents were given minimum care and had to work for long hours as virtual slaves. The conditions in both were made very unattractive in order to discourage the poor from seeking help (Rao, 1994).

Critique and Implications

The poor were not considered the state's responsibility by liberal economists such as Malthus. In his famous *Essay on the Principle of Population* (1798), Malthus said that population tends to increase more rapidly than food supplies. He said that the poor had no moral right to relief as they diminish the share of the more industrious and more worthy. He observed that charity increases population without increasing food for them. Charity would make people lazy and dependent and only increase population whereas poverty, according to him, was a natural means for population control (Rao, 1994). This liberal ideology brought a shift from state-sponsored welfare to organised voluntary charity. In 1834, the New Poor Law was enacted whereby public assistance was not considered a right and government was not responsible for employment (Leiby, 1987).

Although many changes have been made in the Elizabethan Poor Laws -- as thinking about society and social welfare evolved -- they remain, to this day, the basis for much government social welfare policy throughout the Western world. Such features as distinguishing between the deserving and undeserving poor, restricting eligibility, and so on, continue to be used in many parts of the world (Macarov, 1995).

During the Great Depressions of the 1930s, massive changes were brought about in social welfare programmes throughout the world, mostly in the form of increased government responsibilities, as individuals or private agencies were unable to deal with the massive problems. Government activities began to overshadow the work of all voluntary and public organisations because only the national government had the resources and the structure to attack the widespread problems. This was the beginning of the concept of welfare state. After the Second World War, in England, Beveridge published *Social Insurance and Allied Services,* generally known as the Beveridge Report, in 1942. This document provided seminal ideas that affected thinking about welfare in many countries (Macarov, 1995).

Liberalism and Democracy

Historical Context of Origin and Development

With science replacing religion and ideology, the ideas of individual initiative and individual control became the basis for a new ideology – liberalism. With the change in the predominant production process from agricultural to industrial, the rising industries required labour that was tied to the land. It became imperative for the rising industrial groups to displace the nobility from the seats of power and to displace the clergy as the legitimiser of the rule of the nobility and the kings. The new social class of bankers, traders and manufacturers, whose power lay only in the control of moveable property, challenged the political control by the landowning aristocracy. Democracy or the concept of people's rule, emerged to delegitimise feudalism and limit the king's powers (*The World Book Encyclopedia,* 1988).

The liberal ideology laid the foundation of the vast socio-political changes, which began as 'bourgeois revolution' in different European countries. In England, the revolution of 1688 established the supremacy of parliament, implying that the final authority in political matters belonged to the people and not the royalty. However, during the 1760s, the British Government began to tax North American colonists even though the colonists were given no representation in the British Parliament. The latter refused to pay and war broke out in 1775. This war resulted in American Independence and Declaration of Rights in 1781 (*World History*, 1996).

The people of 18th century France had long suffered from exploitation in the feudal system. The majority suffered from high taxes, bad harvests, and limitations on their freedom (*World History*, 1996). The French Revolution with the slogan of "liberty, fraternity and equality" resulted in the Declaration of the Rights of Man and of the Citizen in 1789 (United Nations, 1992). It did not make France a democracy, but limited the king's powers. The liberal revolutions of England, USA and France led to the establishment of many governments based on rule by law and by the consent of the governed.

These revolutions laid the foundation of 'modern nation-states', based on the liberal ideology, which accompanied a transition of power to the industrialist commercial group (Ram, 1999). A nation is a group of people who share a common culture, history or language, and have a feeling of national unity. A state is an area of land whose people have an independent government. A nation-state exists if a nation and a state have the same boundaries. Emergence of nation-states led to the development of an ideology of nationalism that gives people a sense of belonging and pride, and a willingness to make sacrifices for their nation. However, nationalism also produces rivalry and tension between nations. Desires for national glory and military conquest lead to wars. Extreme nationalism resulted in racial hatred and in persecution of a minority group, for example, the Jewish holocaust in Nazi-ruled Germany. Both, Hitler of Germany and Mussolini of Italy used nationalism in demanding extreme loyalty of their people and set out to conquer the world, which led to the Second World War. After the war, nationalism led to many African and Asian colonies demanding for self-government (*The World Book Encyclopedia*, 1988).

The liberal ideology facilitated the Industrial Revolution that began in England in the 1700s, with raw materials from its colonies. It spread to other parts of Europe and to North America in the early 1800s. It created an enormous increase in the production of many kinds of goods, some resulting from the introduction of power-driven machinery and the development of factory organisation (*The World Book Encyclopedia*, 1988).

Ideals, Rationale and Goals for Social Change

Liberalism sought to limit the range of political authority and tried to develop a system of fundamental right for freedom to hold private property, not subject to invasion by the state. Classical economists like Adam Smith were deeply concerned about liberty for individuals and saw their classical economic doctrines as the best way to ensure it. He arranged the ideals of economic liberalism in his book *The Wealth of Nations* (1776), which had a strong influence on development of capitalism or free enterprise. According to him, supply and demand will regulate not only prices of goods but also the incomes of those who produce the goods. The important thing is that no one should interfere in any way with the free operation of supply and demand, self-interest and competition. This is the source of the term laissez-faire (Macarov, 1995). He urged the governments to stop interfering in trade and provide social benefits for heavy losers, in the form of welfare, to prevent them from revolting (Boguslaw, 1992).

Early liberals favoured constitutional government but distrusted democracy. They tried to restrict the exercise of political power to members of the property-owning middle class (*The World Book Encyclopedia,* 1988). The capitalists created powerful lobbies to control the democratic institutions (Sharma, 1998). Today democracy implies faith in human potentialities, which brings into use the human resources that are now so tragically wasted. It emphasises a system of governance for groups, organisations or governments in which the members participate in the decision making of that collectivity. Democracy demands accountability of that collectivity to its members (Creighton, 1992).

According to John Dewey, democracy is the faith that the process of experience is more important than any special result attained, so that special results achieved are of ultimate value only as they are used to enrich and order the ongoing process. All ends and values that are cut off from the ongoing process become arrests or fixations (cited by Geiger, 1947). The basic features of democracy today are, freedom of expression, free election, majority rule and minority rights, political parties, division of power, constitutional government and private organisations (*The World Book Encyclopedia,* 1988).

Representative multiparty democracy, single party democracy and participatory or direct democracy are different types of democracy being practised. Nations which practise multiparty democracy, are usually called liberal democracies, such as India. China practices single party democracy, where people do not choose between parties but between candidates. In participatory democracy, decisions are taken communally by those affected by them (Giddens, 1993).

Critique and Implications

Liberalism substituted economic relations for traditional communal bonds, neglecting such values as solidarity, love, affection and a sense of community. Magnanimity, responsibility, patience, compassion and humility were ridiculed, and egoism, acquisitiveness and disrespect were promoted as the new ideals (Fink, 1981). Classes became groups of people, one of which can appropriate the labour of another, owing to the different places they occupy in the economic system. It also resulted in understanding physical labour as participating in production and mental labour as enjoying its fruits (Rao, 1997). As opposed to the slaves and the serfs, the labourers were formally free, yet they were fully dependent upon the capitalists, economically, as they must sell their labour to them (Belov, 1986). According to Karl Marx, the capitalist relations of production were as exploitative as the feudal ones, but liberal ideas of individuality had the effect of concealing this fact (Fink, 1981).

The determinant of status in class-stratification is supposed to be individual merit, which has to be proved by competition. However, this does not happen in practice, since the majority have already been deprived of the means of production and, therefore, also of the fruits of production (Kappen, 1994). Industrialisation took manufacturing out of the home. Most workers of industries lived and worked under harsh conditions. Factory wages were purposely kept low, to keep them working (*The World Book Encyclopedia*, 1988).

Freedom was thus reduced to freedom for the minority to oppress the majority (Belov, 1986). Property and race qualifications for voting disappeared only gradually. During the second half of the 19th century, the working classes demanded and received greater political rights. Women could vote only since the 1920s (*The World Book Encyclopedia,* 1988). Representative democracy has led to the rise of an oligarchy whose leaders have interests that differ from those of the ordinary citizens, whom they represent (Creighton, 1992). Participatory democracy is found to be effective only in groups with 500 or fewer members (Marshall, 1994).

Utilitarianism and Social Darwinism

Historical Context of Origin

The liberalist ideology and the Industrial Revolution made European nationalism aggressive and expansionist, promoting international trade and colonisation of Asian and African countries. The European nation-states, in vantage positions to increase the productive capacities of their own economies, acquired command over the resources as also the people of the colonies, and thus reinforced their home economies. The production machines in the imperial nation-states were devoted increasingly to industrial goods, while other essential commodities and raw materials were obtained from the colonies (Sharma, 1998). The ideologies of utilitarianism and Social Darwinism justified such cross-country exploitation.

Ideals, Rationale and Goals for Social Change

Utilitarianism was the visible core of 19th century liberalism. The principle of utility, the notion that every possible action of a human being is either taken or not, depending upon whether it is seen as resulting in either pleasure or pain, was the basis for this ideology, modelled on the physical sciences. Using a 'rational' model, it announced that by pursuing one's own pleasure and avoiding pain, each person would maximise happiness for everyone. The assumption was that society was simply a collection of separate individuals operating in their individual self-interests and government action or interference constituted a disservice to these individuals and should be rejected on scientific grounds (Boguslaw, 1992).

Charles Darwin, influenced by Malthus' famous essay on population, was struck by the fact that under circumstances of insufficient sustenance for all, favourable variations would tend to be preserved and unfavourable ones to be destroyed. From this he developed the concept of survival of the fittest, as published in *On the Origin of Species*, in 1859. Social Darwinism attempted to apply Darwin's theory of natural selection and the struggle for existence to the evolution of human society (Macarov, 1995). Progress then became the key idea in the 19th century theories of social evolution, and evolutionism was the common core shared by the most influential social theories of the century (*Britannica.com*, 2000).

It was inferred from Social Darwinism that successful business-people were responsible for their own status and that the unsuccessful were getting what they deserved. In this view, organisations that show a profit are *ipso facto* both successful and desirable, without regard to how the profit is produced, and those that cannot show a profit thereby indicate their unfitness to survive. Whatever is has proved its fitness by continuing to exist; whatever exists is fittest to exist. Everything, therefore, is as it should be, and nothing should be changed. In this manner, Social Darwinism led to the practice of defending the status quo. Any attempt to alter or disturb its workings by aiding the unfit was worse than futile as it was considered an attempt to thwart the will of God or nature. In addition, it was also considered immoral to help the unfit at the expense of the fit (Macarov, 1995).

Evolutionary thought also dominated the new field of social and cultural anthropology in the second half of the 19th century according to which contemporary societies were classified on an evolutionary scale, from "savage" through "barbarian" to "civilized." Tylor postulated an evolution of religious ideas from animism through polytheism to monotheism. Morgan classified societies on the basis of the level of technology, or sources of subsistence, which he connected with the kinship system. He assumed that monogamy was preceded by polygamy, and patrilineal descent by matrilineal descent (*Britannica.com*, 2000).

Social Darwinism divided people into hierarchical dichotomies of 'worthy and not worthy' and 'deserving and non-deserving', which led to dichotomies of 'haves and have nots'. The Protestant ethic made the negatively defined seem immoral and the liberalists made them appear deviant as they are presumably uninterested in competing with others in the open market. They were justifiably refused the fundamental life support resources and were even deemed expendable (Ramsay, 1999). The dichotomies of 'primitive' and 'civilised', 'backward' and 'advanced' and 'superstitious' and 'scientific' justified colonisation. After the colonies were given independence, they were classified as 'underdeveloped' and the ex-colonisers as 'developed' (Gardener and Lewis, 1996).

Critique and Implications

Utilitarianism has been attacked for creating a world of possessive individualism. It assumes the existence of individuals and abstract rules without a society that shapes them (Marshall, 1994). Individualism became essential for the economic growth, social values being considered secondary to the creation and satisfaction of wants. Individualism, therefore, got defined as a political and social ideology, that places high value on the self-directed, self-contained, and comparatively unrestrained individual or ego. The unlimited pursuit of pleasure is considered the ultimate right of every person, thus transmuting selfishness into a universal virtue (Pereira, 1997). Kappen (1994) explains that individualism emphasises 'individual' as an exclusive concept, defined in opposition to other individuals. It is different from 'person', which is an inclusive concept, defined only in relation to other persons.

Social Darwinism became a rationalisation for racism and/or prejudice against ethnic groups of various kinds. The inferiority of some groups was proved by the very fact that their economic status was low, or their educational attainments inferior, or their social status undesirable. This aspect of Social Darwinism resulted in the displacement of "equality" as the basic American goal by "equality of opportunity". As equality obviously had not been achieved it was dismissed as anti-evolutionary and, therefore, unnatural. Instead, the US offers everyone equality of opportunity. If some cannot take advantage of such opportunity, it can be only because of their own deficiencies -- or more bluntly, their inferiority. It is also called blaming the victim (Macarov, 1995).

Western sociologists and economists in the 1950s and 1960s elaborated modernisation theories, which implied a covertly Western-centred evolutionism insofar as they assumed that poor countries had stagnated on a relatively low level of development and could and should develop, or modernise, in the direction of a Western-type society. Modernisation theories have been criticised for their lack of attention to international power relations, in which the richer countries dominate the poorer ones. These relations have been brought into the centre of attention by more recent theories of international dependency or, in Immanuel Wallerstein's terms, the "world capitalist system" (*Britannica.com*, 2000).

Socialism

Historical Context of Origin and Development

The idea of collective ownership of property dates at least from the time of ancient Greece. Around 300 BC, the Greek philosopher Plato proposed that a ruling class own everything in common, putting the welfare of the state above all personal desires (*The World Book Encyclopedia,* 1988). During the French Revolution also, the ideology emerged that human society can be organised on the basis of common ownership of economic resources by the direct producers or the workers (Marshall, 1994). As the contradictions and limitations of liberal humanism became evident, they gave rise to the experiment of socialist humanism, in the latter half of the 19th century (Ikeda, 1998).

Perception of People and Social Problems

Karl Marx, a scientific socialist, also called the "father of socialism", examined the four different forms of societies covering the whole span of human history: primitive communism, ancient slave society, feudalism and capitalism. At each of the last three stages, there was inequality of classes. The change from one stage to another was in response to newer modes of production and facilitated by conflict between classes (cited by Gore, 1993).

Ideals, Rationale and Goals for Social Change

People reacted to the competitive and unequal nature of the capitalist society in different ways. The utopian socialists idealised a new order organised around small communities based on fellowship, harmony and altruism as against bourgeois individualism (Szelenyi, 1992).

Marx believed that as capitalism enters its advanced stage, and enters the international scene, workers across the world will be forced to unite, overthrow capitalism and replace it with socialism. He predicted that private property would be abolished, the forces of production would be nationalised in the hands of the state, rights of inheritance would be eliminated, and so on. He referred to the higher stage of socialism as communism. The democratic socialists questioned Marx's scientific socialism. According to them, democracy was the most important feature of socialist society (Szelenyi, 1992).

Approach to Social Change

Marxism asserted the basic unity of theory and practice by finding that the function of the former was to serve the latter. Theory was always, in fact, expressive of class interests, consequently, philosophy should be transferred into a tool for furthering the class struggle, not abstractly to discover the truth but concretely to forge the intellectual weapons of the proletariat was philosophy's dominant task (*Encyclopaedia Britannica*, 2001).

The paradigm of development as adopted by the socialist countries was largely the same as that of the capitalistic world. Production and consumption of goods and services had been accepted as the measure of development. The decision regarding production, use and distribution, however, was not in the arena of market forces but under the command of the political system (Sharma, 1998).

In the first half of the 19th century, the workers started creating trade or labour unions and national and international federations of unions, through which they struggled against the capitalist system. Their political ideal was the abolition of private property in land and machinery and its replacement by communal ownership and control of all the factors of production and distribution (Fink, 1981). During the late 1800s, several socialist political parties were formed in Europe and North America. In time, these parties became united in an international organisation with a single set of beliefs inspired by the writings of Karl Marx. Between 1890 and 1914, the socialist parties nearly won control of government in several countries. However, after the First World War, the international socialist movement collapsed. Following the Russian Revolution, the revolutionary socialists founded new parties, called communist parties (*The World Book Encyclopedia,* 1988).

Critique and Implications

A review of literature by Szelenyi (1992) shows that the socialist countries secured a number of major achievements such as industrialisation, advancement of science and technology, full employment, price stability, women's labour force participation, expanded child care facilities, improved educational, health and welfare systems, strengthened military power, and so on.

After achieving decrease in inequalities in income in the first stage, the second stage of the experiment of socialism was marked by the emergence of new privileges and crystallisation of new inequalities. An intellectual or bureaucratic elite emerged under state socialism to take the place of the old capitalist class. They did not formally own the means of production but they controlled the production of goods and the allocation of valued resources while managing others (Grusky and Takata, 1992). Cleaver (1993) observed that socialism practised in these countries was authoritarian and not democratic, and was conceptualised as a unified and homogenous social system and not open to social, cultural and ethnic diversity. In Eastern Europe, communist governments were overthrown in 1989. In 1991, the Soviet Union was broken up.

The subaltern studies emerged in the early 1980s in a dissident-Left milieu, where sharp criticism of orthodox Marxist practice and theory was still combined with the retention of a broad socialist and Marxian horizon. There were obvious affinities with the radical-populist moods of the 1960s and 1970s, and specifically with efforts to write 'histories from below'. The common ground lay in a combination of enthusiastic response to popular, usually peasant, rebellions, with growing disillusionment about the organised Left parties, revised versions of orthodox Marxist ideology, and the bureaucratic state structures of 'actually existing socialism'. Today, its dominant thrust is focused on critiques of

Western-colonial power-knowledge, with non-Western 'community consciousness' as its valorised alternative (Sarkar, 1997).

Human Rights

Historical Context of Origin and Development

The ideology of human rights owes its evolution to the emerging middle class quest for political and civil liberties, within European civilisations, since the 17th century. In the 18th century, the concept of natural rights as political rights got deeply grounded. Then the demand was against despotism, arbitrariness and the political disenfranchisement of those who held different opinions (Kamenka, 1978).

Increased enmity among European nations led to the First World War in 1914. After this war, the economy of the European nations, both the victors and the ones defeated, had collapsed. However, the US had become a rich nation since it did not directly suffer from the war and also because of the enormous trade it carried on during the war period. For their rehabilitation, the European nations borrowed heavily from the US. In 1929, when the US was hit by economic depression, it could no more lend money to the European nations. Consequently, the European industries came to a standstill. Collapse of democratic governments led to a rise of military dictatorship in some countries such as Italy, Germany and Spain. The aggressive and expansionist policies of these countries led to the Second World War. The economic losses during this war, too, were enormous, which compelled them to end colonisation. However, the US emerged as a superpower this time also (*Imperialism and Indian Freedom Struggle*, 1998).

After the Second World War, the United Nations was set up in 1945 with the aim of preventing future wars. Development of human rights instruments and promoting their implementation, round the world, is one of the activities undertaken towards this aim. For the first time in the history of humankind, the human rights instruments gave a hope that the basic needs of every human on the globe would be fully met (Sharma, 1998).

Perception of People and Social Problems

A United Nations Report (1992) explains that the denial of human rights and fundamental freedoms is not only an individual and personal tragedy, but also creates conditions of social and political unrest, sowing the seeds of violence and conflict within and between societies and nations.

Ideals, Rationale and Goals for Social Change

The Judeo-Christian ideology influenced the Western idea of revolutions and human rights as requiring a transcendent moral order to be set against the mundane municipal order in which we live, and insisting that the confrontation takes place in this world (Kamenka, 1978). Human rights could be generally defined as those rights that are inherent in our nature and without which, we cannot live as human beings. According to the United Nations (1992), human rights and fundamental freedoms allow us to fully develop and use our human qualities, our intelligence, our talents and our spiritual and other needs. They are basic and fundamental for humankind's increasing demand for a life in which the inherent dignity and worth of each human being will receive respect and protection. Human rights are described in broad terms to be general and universally applicable, from which specific rights are supposed to be derived.

The ideology of human rights comprises of values of human dignity drawn from secular humanism; freedom drawn from liberalism; participation drawn from democracy; and equality drawn from socialism. The development of human rights has been one of evolution. A concern for civil and political rights, which was the initial spur to the conceptualisation of human rights in the 18th century, was gradually matched by a demand for economic, social and cultural rights. In the 1990s, a third generation of rights was recognised as a legitimate universal aspiration for peace, development and a clean environment, protected from destruction (United Nations, 1992).

Human Rights Instruments

Declarations

A declaration is a formal and solemn human rights instrument, enunciating general principles and broad obligations. It is not a binding instrument and does not impose specific obligations on member states. However, depending on the solemnity and significance of a declaration, it may be expected that members of the international community will abide by it (United Nations, 1992). The Universal Declaration of Human Rights of 1948, with its 30 Articles, drew together ideas shared by many political, cultural, and religious traditions, to set out the treatment, that everyone in the world would be able to expect, as a member of the human family.

Covenants

Two covenants (agreements) were derived from the Universal Declaration, in 1966, which set out internationally recognised standards against which human rights violations can be judged: The International Covenant on Civil and Political Rights and the International Covenant on Economic, Social and Cultural Rights. The Covenant on Civil and Political Rights is the capitalist contribution that focusses on the liberal ideology. It includes right to life; freedom from torture, slavery, servitude, forced labour and unlawful arrest; freedom of movement, thought, opinion, conscience and religion; and so on.

The Covenant on Economic, Social and Cultural Rights is the contribution of the socialist lobby, which recommends state intervention for redistribution of resources. It emphasises the right to government provision for basic necessities such as technical and vocational guidance and training programmes, policies and techniques to achieve steady economic, social and cultural development and full and productive employment. The Covenant on Economic, Social and Cultural Rights has not been ratified by the US and, therefore, not received as much attention as the Covenant on Civil and Political Rights (Lobo, 1991).

Convention

A convention is an international agreement containing provisions to promote or protect specific human rights or fundamental freedoms. Conventions are open for signature and ratification by states. A convention is legally binding upon the states which have become parties to it, by ratification (United Nations, 1992).

Critique and Implications

The ideology of human rights tends to be individualistic, based more or less on liberal humanism. The term itself implies that the individual takes priority over the community. According to Marx, the rights that became fashionable at the end of the 18th century were the rights of the egoistic human being, of human being separated from other human beings and the community (Minogue, 1978). Secondly, human rights ignore the social stratification and dynamics of marginalisation between groups due to which these rights are denied to a large number of people, in the first place. The rights are thus ahistorical. As a result, only those who are already better off, can obtain their human rights, although the rights are worded with the assumption of equality between the haves and the have nots (Lobo, 1991). Moreover, rights are proclaimed for which nobody is, or could be responsible. Talk of rights seems to imply an absoluteness that is unsustainable in theory and dangerous in practice. Mutuality between rights and responsibilities is necessary to allow scope for negotiating some reasonable balance of responsibilities between one group and another (Shankardass, 1997).

Summary Chart 2

Western Ideologies in their Historical and Societal Context and Implications

Historical Stage	*Societal Context*	*Ideologies*	*Implications*
ANCIENT PERIOD: Up to 400s	Agricultural and horticultural society, slavery system	Greek ideologies of Socrates, Plato and Aristotle	Spread of Greek ideologies by the Roman Empire
MEDIEVAL PERIOD: 400s to 1600s	Monarchies Feudalism	Judeo-Christian ideology	Dominant religious force in the Western world
	Renaissance	Secular humanism	Revival of importance of human beings
	Reformation	Protestantism	Promotion of individualism and work ethics
MODERN PERIOD: 1600s to 1950s	Age of Enlighten-ment	Rationalism	Promotion of scientism
		Welfarism	Deserving poor distinguished from undeserving poor
	Nation-states Class system International trade	Liberalism Democracy	Promotion of freedom, capitalism and international trade

Contd...

Contd...

Historical Stage	*Societal Context*	*Ideologies*	*Implications*
MODERN PERIOD: 1600s to 1950s	Colonisation Industrial Revolution	Utilitarianism Social Darwinism	Justification of colonisation Industrial Revolution Spread of capitalism in most parts of the world
		Socialism	Promotion of equality
	After the World Wars End of colonisation	Human rights	Further promotion of individualism and liberalism

Module 2

Western History of Ideologies of Social Work Profession

TEACHER/LEARNER OBJECTIVES

The module on 'Western History of Ideologies of Social Work Profession' may have the following teacher/learner objectives:

1. Analyse how the Western modern ideologies have led to requirements of a profession such as social work in terms of secularisation of help and importance of scientific knowledge, formal education and specialisations.
2. Examine the liberalistic context of predominance of the clinical approach in social work profession in the US and its implications for support from the capitalists and the state.
3. Understand the influence of the systems theory on social work and the emergent ecological social work approach.

4. Examine the types, levels, roles and process of social work practice.
5. Study the professionalisation of the normative and the cognitive attributes of social work in the US and its implications for the profession becoming an end in itself.

ORGANISED AND SCIENTIFIC CHARITY

Historical Context of Origin and Development

Charitable work or philanthropy flourished in industrialised countries from the 19th century onwards. Such work led to organisations being formed by the middle and wealthy classes to provide relief and welfare to the poor and less privileged, whether to meet their material needs, or to help them meet their needs themselves. It was a limited way of transferring resources from the rich to the poor (Voluntary Action Network India, no date).

In the latter half of the 19th century, there was a growing realisation that charity needs to be organised to reduce cost and made scientific or secular and humanitarian instead of religion-based. The two types of organised and scientific charity approaches developed were Charity Organization Society (COS) and settlement houses. The first COS was founded in England in 1869. In the US, the first COS was set up in 1877, following the model in England. In 1889, the first settlement house was set up in the US. A National Conference of Charities and Corrections was initiated in the US, in 1874, to bring attention to the organisation and management of state and local custodial institutions, voluntary charity and other philanthropic agencies (Leiby, 1987).

Ideals, Rationale and Goals for Intervention

Scientific charity was based in secular humanism and rationalism. By 'scientific' is meant that helpers should base their efforts on the facts of the situation and that helping should be rational, with a clear idea of means and ends (Leiby, 1987). It also accepted Social Darwinism as an ideological base for its activities (Macarov, 1995). The goal was the moral improvement and effective regulation of 'disorganised' and stigmatised working class people (Payne, 2000).

Benefactors and their Approach to Intervention

COSs

The COS considered friendly visit a substitute of alms, and became a major model for dealing with the urban poor. The main principles of the COS were detailed investigation of the applicant, close cooperation between various relief agencies under a board of their representatives and extensive use of voluntary workers for family visits. The duties of the friendly visitors in a district were to visit those in indigent circumstances to advise them with respect to their business, education of their children, economy of their housing, and to administer encouragement or admonition. Necessities were provided in small amounts – just enough to meet the immediate needs (Brieland, 1987).

The relation between the visitor and the client may have been personal but not 'friendly', in the sense of the informal, natural cohesiveness of peers sharing similar social and cultural backgrounds. The visitors saw in their clients less an equal or potential equal, than an object of character reformation. According to the former, the latter's unfortunate and lowly condition resulted from ignorance or deviations from middle-class values and patterns of life-organisation such as temperance, industriousness, family cohesiveness, frugality, foresight, and moral restraint (Lubove, 1965, cited by Brieland, 1987). The COSs stressed religious values. A major goal was to save "the miserable from the sins of poverty". The COSs are regarded as the forerunners of modern casework (Brieland, 1987).

Settlement Houses

The functioning of the settlement houses stood in contrast to that of the COSs. Staff members were linked to the community because they lived there. Rather than provide charity they sought to help the communities of immigrants with all their problems in a geographic area. They used persuasion to get local politicians to provide basic services to the areas they served. They used group work, community organisation and advocacy methods to attend to working conditions and economic reforms (Brieland, 1987).

Critique and Implications

Scientific charity found little support among rural townspeople, who were likely to regard the plight of the urban poor as punishment for sin, rum, and Roman Catholicism. The big-city poor people were likely to affirm traditional and sentimental charity as a sign of goodwill. Shopkeepers and skilled workers were likely to look to politics or unions as a solution to their problems. The majority of the urban business and professional class was likely to be complacent, or if concerned, they were likely to support doctrinaire Social Darwinists or socialists, who seemed to get at the roots of problems. It was the latter group who felt the importance of empirical knowledge base and formal education of the functionaries of the COSs and settlement houses for imparting such knowledge, leading to establishment of schools of social work (Leiby, 1987).

BEGINNING OF SOCIAL WORK EDUCATION

Social work education in the US emerged from three parallel and related institutional developments during the last half of the 19th century: (1) the development of social sciences as academic disciplines, (2) the establishment of the National Conference of Charities and Corrections, and (3) the establishment of privately sponsored women's colleges and co-educational public universities (Newcomer, 1959, cited by Austin, 1997). Moreover, the existing improvements in medicine gave credibility to the cause of scientifically based helping professions such as social work (Leiby, 1987).

Mary Richmond made a compelling plea for a training school in applied philanthropy at the 1897 meeting of the National Conference on Charities and Corrections. Under her leadership, in 1898, the New York COS established the first school of social work, called the Summer School of Philanthropic Work (later to become the Columbia University School of Social Work), which began as a six week summer school. The first full-scale school of social work was the Institute for Social Work Training, established in Amsterdam in 1899 (Kendall, 2000).

The turn of the century marked a perceptible shift towards secularisation of welfare, which de-emphasised the connection to charity (Reamer, 2001). In 1900, the term 'charity' was replaced by 'social welfare', 'friendly visitors' was replaced by 'social workers', and 'philanthropy' by 'social work'. In time, 'social welfare' came to refer to agencies and programmes and 'social work' to an occupation in such agencies (Leiby, 1987). By 1910, professional education programmes were firmly established in several European and North American countries (Kendall, 1998).

CLINICAL SOCIAL WORK

Historical Context of Origin and Development

Professional social workers in the US might have focussed on policy and administration, as they did, to some extent, in England. However, the legislators and executives in the US were not inclined to look to professional social workers for advice about their decisions and how to implement them (Leiby, 1987).

In 1917, Mary Richmond published a book, *Social Diagnosis*, which provided techniques for assessing the situation of the poor. She drew largely on the rhetoric of law: collecting and sifting "evidence", about "cases" and helping "clients" (Leiby, 1987). In 1922, she published *What is Social Work,* which defined the casework method. Leadership of caseworkers in development of scientific knowledge base as well as specialised skills, techniques and functions, led to their subsequent dominance in the profession (Hopps and Pinderhughes, 1987).

In 1935, the Social Security Act was enacted which recognised the need for a welfare system capable of handling social problems that often resulted from rapid industrialisation. This Act took care of the financial problems of poor and other needy people. Coping with resolving the emergent social problems was believed to be beyond the scope and capacity of a largely volunteer-sponsored and organised charity system. The market for professional social workers was agency boards or executives who wanted people who could do casework in a knowledgeable and expert way and supervise untrained people on the job (Leiby, 1987). Social workers believed that they had the means to provide solutions to the dysfunctional patterns that could not be cured by money, so they turned towards their counselling roles. Numerically and technologically casework thus has dominated the profession, most of the times. Also known as clinical social work, this approach drew heavily from the psychological sciences, particularly psychoanalytic theory and methodology (Humphreys and Dinerman, 1984).

In the aftermath of the Great Depression, an important split emerged in social work's basic values and orientation towards helping. A significant portion of the profession continued to concentrate on therapeutic work, with an emphasis on individual change. In contrast were the practitioners committed to advancing pubic welfare. Their work was conducted in public agencies, charged primarily with serving the poor, disabled, and those otherwise in need. Following the Second World War, the relative tranquility associated with peacetime and domestic calm turned the values attention of both the nation and its professionals inward. Pursuit of individual well-being became more compelling than pursuit of the public good. Clinical social work gained control of the profession until the turbulent 1960s. Since the 1980s again the majority of the social workers devoted their careers to providing counselling and casework services to individuals and families. Relatively few social workers were employed in community organising, advocacy or policy positions (Reamer, 2001).

Benefactors and their Motives

Some of the graduates from the new women's colleges were interested in occupational careers concerned with the oppression and exploitation of women and children and with conditions facing immigrant families in crowded cities. Casework was viewed as particularly appropriate for altruistic women, consistent with popular assumptions about the domestic "caring" responsibilities of women in general (Austin, 1997).

Perception of People and Social Problems

According to the clinical social work approach, some people cannot adjust to the larger forces due to psycho-social problems. Clients are considered deviants with a dysfunctional condition (Parsons, Jorgensen and Hernandez, 1994). In 1984, the National Association of Social Workers (NASW) defined clinical social work as professional application of social work theory and methods to the treatment and prevention of psycho-social dysfunction, disability or impairment including emotional and mental disorders (Swensen, 1995).

Ideals, Rationale and Goals for Intervention

Social work emerged in the context of Western capitalism. The profession's values, particularly those focussed on self-determination and right to privacy and informed consent, have been influenced by Western individualistic political views (Reamer, 2001). Secular, scientific and liberal ideologies influenced professional social work. Casework principles valued acceptance, non-condemning attitudes, confidentiality and controlled emotional involvement (Mathew, 1987).

Approach to Intervention

Clinical social work is a specialised form of direct social work intervention with individuals, groups and families that takes place, for the most part, in the worker's office (Barker, 1994).

The first Working Definition of Social Work Practice, developed by NASW, in 1956, stated that social work practice is the responsible, conscious, disciplined use of self in a relationship with an individual or groups. Through this relationship, the practitioner facilitates interaction between the individual and his or her social environment. This definition did not cover community organisation, as it had a clinical orientation. Clinical social work services today include assessment, diagnosis and treatment, including psychotherapy and counselling, client-centred advocacy, consultation and evaluation (Swensen, 1995).

Critique and Implications

The individualistic approach isolated people from their family and community context, which resulted in blaming the victim. Clinical social work continued to pull away from the poor in favour of dealing with those problems amenable to a counselling mode of treatment. Social work was accused of seeking a clientele with a higher standing in an effort to raise its own position in society (Humphreys and Dinerman, 1984). Casework was critiqued to be contributing to the oppression of the poor and other disadvantaged people. It was seen as reducing the motivation of the oppressed to engage in social protest, which led to the ecological approach in the 1970s (Swensen, 1995).

ECOLOGICAL SOCIAL WORK

Historical Context of Origin and Development

The clinical paradigm in social work continued to dominate the profession until the 1960s. The goal of professionalisation was seriously questioned during this time when some social workers argued that social action and social change were the true goals of social work practice and that such goals were incompatible with professionalisation and social status (Humphreys and Dinerman, 1984). The period marked a new threshold in social work's efforts to grapple with the profession's values, with their inexorable focus on social values and social justice issues (Reamer, 2001).

Western modern ideologies have tended to be linear, atomistic, and analytical. Since the 1970s, the systems model of conceptualisation has been changing the perspectives in several disciplines, including social work. A move towards transactional and synthesis oriented social work brought an ecological orientation to social work practice, that was integrated, holistic and generalist (Bartlett, 1970; Goldstein, 1973; Pincus and Minahan, 1973).

Perception of People and Social Problems

In the ecological social work approach, problems are seen as deficits in the environment, as dysfunctional transactions between systems, rather than a disease located within the individual. Problems are not viewed as an attribute of people, these are viewed as an attribute of their social situation. Problems are seen as outcomes of the transaction of many complex variables. The effort to locate a single cause and cure, therefore, is largely abandoned in practice (Hartman and Laird, 1983). It has also sparked off efforts to understand culturally specific populations and to create appropriate frameworks for practice (Pinderhughes, 1995).

In this approach, the target is the social problem, rather than the exclusive rehabilitation of the victims or survivors. The problem's embeddedness from micro to macro systems and linkages between these systems are understood. Oppression and discrimination issues are identified and based on ethnicity, gender, class, age and sexual orientation. Victims of social problems are understood as the most accessible, least powerful, and most easily labelled people (Parsons and others, 1994).

Ideals, Rationale and Goals for Intervention

A systems orientation enhances a holistic view to understand the entirety of the social, psychological and physiological organism and enlarges an appreciation of the creative and adaptive potentialities, not only within the people but also within the systems in which they function (Goldstein, 1973).

The ecological approach stresses that effective social work intervention occurs not only by working directly with clients, but with the familial, social, and cultural factors that impact on their social functioning. The approach also suggests that the traditional methods of social casework, group work, and community practice are dated in that they are largely built on approaches that define the individual as the major cause of social problems (Pardeck, 1996). Methods fragment intervention whereas the ecological approach gives an integrative perspective. It deals with the problem in the natural life situations.

This approach assumes the need to counter negative devaluation of specific client groups by emphasising positivity, normalisation, competency screening and empowerment-based interventions. The approach of normalisation suggests that behaviour cannot be viewed objectively, but must be seen in terms of a person's intentions, motives and reasons (Parsons and others, 1994).

Benefactors and their Motives

In the ecological approach, professional social workers and their employing agencies consider themselves as change agents aiming at systemic change.

Approach to Intervention

The tradition in social work of emphasising both social treatment and social reform emerged as the basis of the ecological approach (Pardeck, 1996). In ecological social work, efforts for change are directed at the interfaces between systems or sub-systems, the goal being the enhancement of relationship between those systems. A feedback model of change is initiated in which interventions are made and tested through the continued monitoring of the system's response (Hartman and Laird, 1983).

The change agent system does the following:

1. Identification of the problem as that which is causing discomfort, impeding functioning, affecting self-realisation, and creating unmet needs, social deprivation and social injustice. Micro-level problems are related to the macro-level issues, which have to do with matters that transcend local environments of individuals.
2. Identification of the client system, which comprises of individuals, groups or communities who are experiencing or likely to experience the problem. Identifying their strength is the next step. The change agent needs the client's sanction to work for it.
3. Identification of the target system that is the system which is causing/affecting the problem/situation, the system which needs to change. If the clients need to change, they are also the target system. The target system may readily agree for change, be indifferent or resist change. The larger and more complex the target system, the less open/flexible its boundaries will be.
4. Decision-making on the goals of change in collaboration with the client system. Different people may be considered targets for different goals at different times.
5. Identification of the action system whose help will be useful to the change agent to achieve the goals for change. For any one problem situation, the change agent may work with several different action systems, to achieve different goals. The action system could be an existing system, a new system or a coordination of several systems.

Strategies are devised which, as far as possible, make use of natural systems and life experiences of the clients (Hartman and Laird, 1983). Family, kinship, friends and neighbourhood comprise the natural systems. The change agent uses collaborative, bargaining and conflictual relationships with the different systems. The clients are provided skills and mobilisation, not treatment (Parsons and others, 1994).

Historical and Contemporary Critique

The ecological paradigm of social work is not as much accepted by social work educators as much as the clinical paradigm is. It is criticised by some for not using the sociological theories adequately to understand human ecology and not recognising that social work practice itself is influenced by its environment (Roberts, 1990).

TYPES, LEVELS, ROLES AND PROCESS OF SOCIAL WORK PRACTICE

Types of Social Work Practice

Social work practice includes remediating that is eliminating existing personal or social problems; restoration, that is rehabilitating those whose social functioning has been impaired; prevention, that is planning, organising and providing services before problems develop, thus enhancing the prospects of social well-being (Barker, 1987).

Levels of Social Work Practice

According to Sheafor, Horejsi and Horejsi (1997), social work intervention can be classified by the size of the client system being addressed, into micro, mezzo and macro levels of practice.

Micro-Level Social Work Practice

Micro-level social work practice focuses on a person's most intimate interactions, such as exchanges between husband and wife, parent and child, close friends and family members. The terms interpersonal helping, direct practice and clinical practice are often interchangeably used with micro level.

Macro-Level Social Work Practice

Macro-level practice may involve work with an organisation, community or even society as a whole. Obviously, macro-level practice also deals with interpersonal relations, but these are the interactions between people who represent organisations or who are members of a work group such as an agency committee or inter-agency task force. When engaged in macro-level practice, the social worker is frequently involved in activities such as administration, fund-raising, testifying on proposed legislation, policy analysis, class advocacy and social resource development.

Mezzo-Level Social Work Practice

Mezzo-level practice is concerned with interpersonal relations that are somewhat less intimate than those associated with family life but more personally meaningful than those that occur among organisational and institutional representatives. Included would be relationships among individuals in a self-help or therapy groups, among peers at school or work, and among neighbours.

Some practice approaches are designed to address more than one intervention level. The generalist perspective requires the social worker to be capable of practice at all the three levels.

Social Worker Roles

Barker (1987) has described the following roles of social workers:

Enabler Role

The enabler role is the responsibility to help the client become capable of coping with situational of transitional stress. Specific skills used in achieving this objective include conveying hope, reducing resistance and ambivalence, recognising and managing feelings, identifying and supporting personal strength, and social assets, breaking down problems into parts that can be solved more readily, and maintaining a focus on goals and the means of achieving them.

Facilitator Role

The facilitator role is the responsibility to expedite the change effort by bringing together people and lines of communications, channelling their activities and resources, and providing them with access to expertise.

Mobiliser Role

The mobiliser role is the responsibility to help people and organisations combine their resources to achieve goals of mutual importance. This is accomplished by bringing clients together, enhancing lines of communication, clarifying goals and steps to achieve them, and devising plans for gaining greater support.

Educator Role

The educator role includes the responsibility to teach clients necessary adaptive skills. This is done by providing relevant information in a way that is understandable to the client, offering advice and suggestions, identifying alternatives and their probable consequences, modelling behaviours, teaching problem solving techniques and clarifying perceptions.

Activist Role

The activist role is the rejection of the so-called objective, neutral or passive stance in favour of taking specific actions on behalf of the client system. These actions may include overt side-taking, making specific recommendations to clients, leading campaigns to change social institutions, or exerting an influence on client value-orientation.

Advocacy Role

The advocacy role is the act of directly representing or defending others, championing the rights of individuals or communities through direct intervention or through empowerment.

Social Work as a Problem-Solving Process

A problem is any question or matter involving doubt, uncertainty or difficulty (Random House, 1992). Problem in social work usage refers to a social-functioning situation in which need-fulfillment of any of the persons or systems involved is blocked and in which the persons involved cannot by themselves remove the block (Johnson, 1983). Following are the types of social situations to which social work practice is addressed: (1) performing life tasks, (2) interaction with resource systems and (3) relating to public issues (Pincus and Minahan, 1973)

Social work with problem-solving is finding a way through feeling, thinking and acting. Process refers to the recurrent patterning of a sequence of change over time and in a particular direction. There is also a tendency to return to earlier stages and a mixing of certain aspects of various stages. Social work as a problem-solving process progresses over time in a cyclical, irreversible manner that is focussed on removing blocks to need fulfillment in social functioning that persons cannot remove with their own resources. Its stages are assessment, planning, action and termination (Johnson, 1983).

ATTRIBUTES OF PROFESSIONS

Concepts of Professional Attributes

The Western modern ideologies thus influenced attributes of a profession: Secular humanism led to secularisation of help. Rationalism and scientism resulted in the importance of empirical knowledge base for social work, which has to be imparted through formal education. Specialisation was an outcome of further progress in knowledge. Individualism led to individual-based diagnosis as well as treatment. The liberal ideology helped the profession achieve support from the corporate sector. The welfare orientation of the professions was suitable to the functioning of the nation-state.

In the present times, professions are a prominent feature of the social landscape because of the complexity of modern society, the explosion of knowledge and the associated need for specialisation, the availability of institutionalised opportunities for advanced education, and the psychic, social, and financial rewards of professional status (Khinduka, 1987).

Further, attributes of a profession are not fixed but rather evolve as society's need for and definition of professions change in response to changing social conditions and values (Humphreys and Dinerman, 1984). In addressing the National Conference of Charities and Correction, in 1915, Abraham Flexner concluded in his paper "Is Social Work a Profession?", that social work was not a profession. He gave the following reasons for this conclusion: (1) it does not have a knowledge base, (2) it is a mediating and not an original agency, dealing with a time-limited phenomenon, and (3) it does not have communicable techniques. Flexner saw social work as essentially a time-limited phenomenon filling temporarily the interstices between and among other professions, until they assumed the tasks performed by social workers as a part of their own responsibility (Humphreys and Dinerman, 1984). Pursuit for professionalism led social workers to work hard for a scientific knowledge base as well as specialised skills, techniques and functions.

According to Greenwood (1981), professionalism is not an either-or phenomenon; the attributes of a profession constitute a continuum and professionalism may be viewed as a scale. Professionalism refers to the degree to which an individual possesses and utilises the knowledge skills and qualifications of a profession and adheres to its values and ethics when serving the client (Barker, 1987).

Classification of Professional Attributes

Greenwood (1981) identified three essential attributes of a profession: cognitive, monopolistic and normative. The following characteristics of a profession can be considered as derivatives of these basic attributes:

Cognitive

1. A systematic body of theories and knowledge
2. Formal education in universities
3. Growth in specialisation

Normative

1. A code of ethical standard with an enforcement mechanism
2. Professional associations

Monopolistic

1. Professional authority
2. Sanction from the society

The conventional approach to the study of professions, listing a set of their ideal typical attributes, is now considered inadequate in explaining the nature of professions. Even established occupations do not meet all such presumed requirements of a profession. On examination, some of what have been regarded as the essential features of professions are revealed as little more than incorporations and legitimations of the prevailing definitions of the proper role of the state, of the market, and of the entrepreneurial system by analysis of the professions (Khinduka, 1987).

Professional Relationships

The social worker's relationship with various systems has the following common elements:

1. The professional relationship is formed for a joint/shared vision/goals (purpose) and not as an end in itself.
2. In professional relationships the social workers devote themselves to the interest of their clients and the needs and aspirations of other people, rather than their own interests.
3. The professional relationship is based on objectivity and self-awareness which allow the social workers to step outside of their own personal troubles and emotional needs and to be sensitive to the needs of others (Pincus and Minahan, 1973).

PROFESSIONALISATION OF SOCIAL WORK

Normative Attributes

Social Work Values and Ethics

Ethics is a system of moral principles and perceptions about right versus wrong and the resulting philosophy of conduct that is practiced by an individual, group, profession or culture (Barker, 1987). When social work practice and education began formally in the US in the late 19th century, practitioners paid more attention to the values and morality of clients than to the morality or ethics of the profession and social workers themselves (Reamer, 1987). The first code of ethics adopted by the NASW in the US (1960) made a series of proclamations concerning, for example, every social worker's duty to give precedence to professional responsibility over personal interests, to respect the privacy of clients, to give appropriate professional service in public emergencies and to contribute knowledge, skills and support to programmes of human welfare (Reamer, 1987). Thus, the code grew out of the rules of acceptable conduct in society. It functioned chiefly to discipline professionals for extreme misconduct, so offered little towards inspiring the profession to a higher ethical level of practice (Walz and Ritchie, 2000). In the late 1970s and 1980s, social workers in the US entered yet another clearly demarcated stage of development with respect to ethics, due largely to the emergence of the new field of applied and professional ethics (Reamer, 2001).

The revised code of ethics published by the National Association of Social Workers in 1996 includes a focus on promoting issues of social justice on behalf of the disadvantaged populations. Its preamble states that,

> The primary mission of the social work profession is to enhance human needs of all people, with particular attention to the needs and empowerment of people who are vulnerable, oppressed, and living in poverty. A historic and defining feature of social work is the profession's focus on individual well-being in a social context and the well-being of society. Fundamental to social work is attention to the environmental forces that create, contribute to, and address problems in living.

This code lists the following broad ethical principles based on social work's core values:

Value: Service
Ethical Principle: Social workers' primary goal is to help people in need and to address social problems.

Value: Social Justice
Ethical Principle: Social workers challenge social injustice.

Value: Dignity and Worth of the Person
Ethical Principle: Social workers respect the inherent dignity and worth of the person.

Value: Importance of Human Relationships
Ethical Principle: Social workers recognise the central importance of human relationships.

Value: Integrity
Ethical Principle: Social workers behave in a trustworthy manner.

Value: Competence
Ethical Principle: Social workers practice within their areas of competence and develop and enhance their professional expertise.

Each state in the US has licensing, registration and statutory certification laws developed to regulate the practice of social work profession. These laws control who can practice the profession of social work, what services social workers can provide, and the titles social workers can present to the public. The voluntary certification programmes developed by NASW and other professional associations also regulate professional practice (Tourse, 1995).

The current stage in the development of social work ethics in the US reflects the dramatic maturation of social workers' understanding of ethical issues. Besides the development of a comprehensive code of ethics, it includes the emergence of a significant body of literature related to malpractice and liability risks in practice and risk management strategies designed to prevent ethics complaints and ethics related lawsuits. As a result of increased litigation against social workers, many social work education programmes, social service agencies and professional organisations are sponsoring special training and education on risk management (Reamer, 2001).

The ethical dilemmas, which social workers face in their work, are summarised by Reamer (2001) into three categories as follows:

1. Services provided to individuals, families and small groups or direct practice face the issues of confidentiality and privacy, informed consent, the limits of clients' right to self-determination, professional paternalism, conflicts of interest and professional boundaries (dual and multiple relationships).
2. Indirect practice or "macro" issues involving social policy, social welfare, social planning, community practice, research and evaluation and administration. Social workers in social policy positions may encounter ethical dilemmas concerning the allocation of limited resources or the coercive use of government authority to address social problems. Social workers in community practice may face ethical dilemmas involving divided loyalties where they feel caught between the interests of community groups that are in conflict. Social workers who conduct research and programme evaluations may encounter ethical dilemmas involving the use of deception in research methodology, protecting research subjects' confidentiality, informed consent and the accurate reporting of results. Social work administrators may face ethical dilemmas related to personnel decisions, contract enforcement, programme funding, marketing, enforcement of sexual harassment regulations, workplace discrimination and employee impairment.

3. Ethical dilemmas with reference to social workers' relationships with their colleagues include situations where social workers encounter unethical conduct or wrongdoing engaged in by colleagues.

Social Work Professional Associations

The Council on Social Work Education (CSWE) was set up in 1952, to set standards under which undergraduate and graduate social work educational institutions function and is the accrediting body for these institutions. All states with social work licensing require applicants to be graduates of schools accredited by CSWE. CSWE publishes the *Journal of Social Work Education*.

In 1955, a National Association of Social Workers (NASW) was set up through the merger of seven organisations. The NASW is the cornerstone of social work profession in the US. It has developed codes of ethics and standards in various areas including personnel practice, clinical practice and continuing education. It publishes the journals *Social Work, Health and Social Work, Social Work in Education, Social Work Research* and *Social Work Abstracts*. It also publishes *NASW News* and *Encyclopedias of Social Work*. In 1992, the NASW incorporated the National Center for Social Policy and Practice, which it established in 1986 as an affiliate. In a membership survey done of the NASW in 1991, 603,000 people were referred to as social workers. The NASW had an estimated membership of 134,200. Of these, 88% were white and 77% were female (Hopps and Collins, 1995).

Cognitive Attributes

Social Work Education

The CSWE Curriculum Policy Statement of 1992 and the Accreditation Standards of 1994 are in force through June 2002, after which they will be superseded by the new Educational Policy and Accreditation Standards. There has been a rapid growth of doctoral programmes in social work. In 1977, the Group for the Advancement of Doctoral Education (GADE) was formed.

Bartlett (1970) noted that family welfare, child welfare, medical social work, psychiatric social work and school social work were the five fields of social work that emerged by the 1920s. According to her, corrections and public welfare were added by the 1940s. The 1960s saw an increasing development of specialisation, whether specific to a method or to a field. The 1969 Curriculum Policy Statement of the CSWE reflected the prevailing laissez-faire approach to specialisation in the US. Although specifying the central areas of content to be covered in graduate education, the statement left schools totally free to design their own curricular specialisations. The 1982 Curriculum Policy Statement of the CSWE, however, confirmed and encouraged the shift within the master's degree programmes towards greater preparation for specialised practice (Siporin, 1984).

Hollis and Taylor (1951) rejected the idea widely held by social workers at that time that casework, group work and community organisations are social work specialisations. They observed the need for social work specialisations to be characterised by functions and not by agency settings. Their objective was to prevent fragmentation of the profession into fields. In specialisations by functions they included advanced practice, administration, supervision, teaching and research. Such specialisations require social workers to explore the whole field of social work from the chosen approach. Later, in 1977, Gordon and Schutz developed a conceptual framework for specialisations across fields. Accordingly, whenever a sufficiently large number of people is found to be affected by a dysfunctional mismatch between their coping capabilities and one or more sectors of the environment, an area of specialisations may be established. Besides the number of people affected, another condition that has to be fulfilled is a body of knowledge which, when applied, leads to demonstrably successful interventions.

Social Work Literature

Social work literature in the US has made remarkable progress since the 1970s in strengthening its knowledge base. The growth of social work journals reflects, both, the increasing specialisation and the centrality of knowledge development, dissemination, and utilisation in the profession. Substantive application of theories, hypotheses, and findings from other disciplines to social work practice and social welfare policy is being done. Social work research has made important methodological gains (Khinduka, 1987). Three journals are published with a focus on social work research: *Journal of Social Service Research*, *Research on Social Work Practice* and *Social Work Research*.

Critique and Implications

According to Weick (1994), in forging its early alliance with a scientific model of knowledge-building, social work was gradually pulled away from its value moorings. The profession paid a price for gaining access to the university by having to accept the positivist epistemology of practice. In doing so, they accepted that university-based scientists and scholars would create the fundamental theory, which professionals would apply to practice. People who were poor or sick, became objects whose knowledge of their own experience was no longer valid. The linkage to science created a new class of 'professionals' and a counterpart class of 'clients'. This has been inconsistent with the social work value of belief in people's innate capacity for growth and the ability to direct the course of their lives. Professionals are thought to possess specialised knowledge about the human condition, which non-professionals do not have. However, human experience as a universal commodity belongs to all of us. No one person or group can be said to exclusively possess this source of knowledge (Weick, 1994).

Professional experts view social services as a work process and not as an interactive process, Wagner (1984) said. He also emphasised that professionalisation does not foreclose the possibility of lay people carrying out social service tasks that do not require specialised qualifications. A positive development would be a flexible system of mutual cooperation in which both paraprofessional and self-help groups enhance and relieve the work of the professional care system.

Khinduka (1987) also noted that a major issue in social work is the uncertainty about the profession's domain and boundaries, underlying which is a yearning for ideological uniformity. He suggests that social work should recognise that ambiguity of domain is not an unmitigated liability; the profession does not become deprofessionalised because of contending ideologies, policy preferences, strategic choices, and special interest sub-groups. A mature profession shares a broad, abstract unity of view and vision, but it is also hospitable to ideological pluralism.

Secularisation of help homogenised problems, devoid of its family and community context. The individual-based diagnosis as well as treatment isolates individuals from their family and community context. Specialisations in social work led to fragmentation of problems that resulted in focus upon symptoms and not causes. Wagner noted that the professionalisation process often leads to a narrowing of the definition of the problem to be solved. This resulted in blaming of the victims and prevented them from revolting.

In professional social work there has been an unstated premise that the social worker was working on behalf of the society, today we would call it the establishment. This is evident from the fact that in the first quarter of the 20th century, social work in the West had allowed the major movements, such as the labour movement, the blacks' movement, and the women's suffrage movement, to pass by without contributing to them (Gore, 1997). Professional social work (PSW) and social movements, both, aim at amelioration of social problems. However, there are vast differences between the two. Social movements are intuitive and commitment-based but PSW is based on formal and scientific education. Social movements have their sources in religious ideologies or modern/postmodern ideologies, whereas PSW has its direct source in Western modern secular ideologies. While social movements analyse the social issues in their historical context, PSW deals with social problems based on immediate needs. Social movements work towards changing the established order, whereas PSW works on behalf of the establishment. The former is, therefore, political and the latter, apolitical. Social movements have historically led to major social changes, while PSW has made marginal changes in individuals, groups and communities. Those in the movements have noted the PSW's capacity to reproduce oppressive social relations under the guise of providing care (Dominelli, 2002) (see Summary Chart 4).

Professionalism is thus critiqued as an ideological bulwark against egalitarianism, unionism and class struggle. By creating allegiance to the agency rather than to people in need and by downplaying issues of hierarchy and class division, the professional model, according to some of its critics, depoliticises social work, and retards the social worker's ability to engage in political struggle and movements (Withorn, 1984, cited by Khinduka, 1987). Left-wingers have criticised it for imposing bureaucratic forms of social control upon poor people living in working class communities and being an oppressive part of the nation-state (Dominelli, 2002). This approach was suitable to the capitalists and the nation-state that, therefore, supported the profession. Social workers became the newer elite and professionalism became an end in itself. Khinduka (1987) observed that professional status offers an individual resources, immunities, privileges, and autonomy. It can be viewed not merely as a calling embodying institutionalised altruism, but as an interest group concerned with professional perquisites, rewards, esteem and influence.

Summary Chart 3

Influence of Western Modern Ideologies on Attributes of A Profession and Implications of Professionalisation of Social Work

Western Modern Ideologies →	*Attributes of a Profession* →	*Implications of Professionalisation of Social Work*
Secular humanism	Secularisation of help	Homogenisation of problems
Rationalism	Scientism	
	Empirical knowledge base	
	Formal education	
	Specialisations	Focus on symptoms and not causes
		Social problems got fragmented
Individualism	Individual-based diagnosis as well as treatment	Individuals got isolated from their family and community context
		Blaming of the victim
Welfarism	Suitable to the nation-states	Prevented people from revolting
Liberalism	Support from the capitalists	Social workers became the newer elites
		Professionalism as an end in itself

Summary Chart 4

Comparison of Professional Social Work with Social Movements

Professional Social Work	*Social Movements*
Formal and scientific education-based	Intuitive and commitment-based
Source in Western modern ideologies of secular humanism, rationalism, humanism and liberalism	Source in religious ideologies and medieval, modern and postmodern ideologies
Deals with problems based on immediate needs	Analyse the issues in their historical context
Works on behalf of the establishment	Work towards changing the established order
Non-political	Political
Makes marginal changes in individuals, groups and communities and has the capacity to reproduce oppressive social relations	Result in major social changes
↓	↓

Amelioration of Social Problems

Module 3

Indian History of Ideologies for Social Change

TEACHER/LEARNER OBJECTIVES

The module on 'Indian History of Ideologies for Social Change' may have the following teacher/learner objectives:

1. Examine the plurality of religious ideologies that have influenced social changes in India, in the context of the Aryan invasion, Turk and Moghul rules and British rule.
2. Understand the development of the Vedic and non-Vedic ideologies in the context of the Aryan invasion and the emergence of the caste system in India, in the ancient period.
3. Examine the influence of Islam in India during the Turk and Moghul rule and the emergence of mysticism of Bhakti and Sufi movements and Sikhism in the medieval period.

4. Study the influence of Christianity and modern ideologies in India, during the British rule, and the emergence of Hindu reform movements and Dalit movements.
5. Understand the Gandhian ideology and Sarvoday movement and nationalism during the freedom movement of India.
6. Analyse the ideology of the Indian Constitution as influenced by the United Nations' Universal Declaration of Human Rights and Indian nationalism and the ideology of voluntary organisations after independence.

ANCIENT PERIOD

Scientific ideology and religious ideology have been closely associated with each other in India, unlike the West, where rationalism started with a repudiation of religion. Religions that originated in India are philosophical speculations and not a direct confrontation of God and human beings. In fact, the two are not clearly distinguished. Human beings are groping towards God and their groping leads them to experience the immortality of their own souls. Their preoccupation is with deliverance of the human soul, which is immortal, from the bondage of the body. Salvation is to realise a deathless condition in which space and time are transcended and in which all links with bodily life have been finally cut away. The attitude is throughout conditioned by an unquestioned and unquestioning belief in reincarnation (Zaehner, 1959).

Vedic Ideology

Historical Context of Origin and Development

The main source of the Vedic religious ideology lies in the *Vedas*, written during 4000 to 1000 BC, by the priestly group of Aryans, namely, Brahmins. The meaning of the *Vedas* is explained in detail in the scriptures called *Upanishads* started in about 900 BC.

Perception of People and of Social Problems

The Indian ethical systems are built on the foundation of metaphysics. Human beings derive values and norms not from the world stuff, nor from the cosmic process, but from within their selves and their relation to other selves and to the cosmos (Mukherji, 1983). According to the Vedic scriptures, *Brahman* is the ultimate reality, which means that everything in the world is but the manifestation of a part of *Brahman*. If *Brahman* is the ultimate reality, and if we are not different from it, birth cannot be our beginning, nor death our end. *Samsara* means transmigration or the flow of *atman* (soul) from beyond birth to beyond death. Thus, *atman* is eternal and birth and death relate to the integration and disintegration of the elements that compose the body (Mahadevan, 1982).

The kind of birth the *atman* takes and the type of enjoyment that falls to its lot are determined by its own past, or *karma*. The term *karma* means work and its result. The law of *karma* states that the sphere of morality is an ordered realm, and is the moral equivalent of the physical law of causality. The sufferings of people are usually understood to be the result of their bad *karma*. Freedom from the cycle of *karma* is called *moksha*, which is not only possible, but is one's ultimate goal and destiny. What prevents the soul from realising it is its own ignorance, which when dispelled through wisdom of the nature of the self, one attains release. *Moksha* is attainable in this life, by achieving an exalted mode of existence, freed from the shackles of egoity and ignorance (Mahadevan, 1982). The liberation of the soul is to be achieved by way of Yoga. The different forms of Yoga are *Jnana* Yoga (philosophy), *Karma* Yoga (work), *Bhakti* Yoga (worship), and *Raj* Yoga (psychic control).

Approach to Social Change

Dharma is the main goal of human beings; it includes virtue, duty and religion. The *ashrama* (life stages) system requires that the *dharma* of the *Grihastha* (householder) is to be hospitable, tend the sick, provide food and medicament for the mute and succour to the relatives in distress and give *dana*. *Dana* means not only gifts to Brahmins and priests but also scattering bounty all around in the form of planting trees, building highways, excavating wells and tanks, and providing places of shelter and treatment, of which all persons and even animals might avail themselves (Bhattacharyya, 1983). The suffering individual also has to be guided to the religious path. Here, the dominant motive for the giver is attainment of religious merit. This is acknowledged and supported by the recipient, who invariably invokes God's blessings for the benefactor. Because of the *karma* theory, both the giver and the receiver tend to be fatalistic and a mediator between the two is not needed (Gore, 1966).

Brahminism

When the Aryans first came to India they were divided into three occupational groups – Brahmins, the priests; Kshatriyas, the warriors; and Vaishyas, the traders. The heredity of occupations was not a recognised principle in the early Vedic age. The darker colour of the native inhabitants of India, whom they conquered, seems to have been the cause of the development of the system of *varna* (colour). The hereditary caste system is supposed to have burgeoned in the later Vedic age. As the *varna* of a person had been assigned to him/her by virtue of his/her birth into it, it was called the *jati* system, which the West translates as caste. Marriages were also permitted only within the caste (Singhal, 1983). The indigenous people and those of mixed descent were labelled as Shudras, the fourth caste and Atishudras (outcastes), who were considered untouchables. These people did all the hard manual labour.

The castes gradually proliferated into sub-castes. While the sub-caste became a source of identity and support for the individual/family, casteism justified hierarchy of castes based on natural and social inferiority of a large number of communities. Sufferings of the lower castes were usually explained by their *karmas*, in this life or the previous lives, and not outside the individuals. No doubts arose about justice in the social arrangement, as though it was God-given (Gore, 1966).

Brahmins dominated the Aryan Vedic religion, emphasising rituals which only they could perform. The non-Brahmins were excluded from reading scriptures and practising rituals. As rituals became important, Brahmins became more dominant. The caste system left no scope whatsoever for choosing an occupation of one's choice, which hampered social progress (*History of India*, 1994).

Jainism and Buddhism

Around sixth to 5th century BC, when the Vedic ideology had lost its original purity, giving rise to ritualism, Buddhism and Jainism challenged the authority of the *Vedas*. These are both atheistic creeds. They were against the caste system and admitted into their fold, all peoples, irrespective of their castes.

Jainism

According to the Jain ideology, *jiva* (soul) exists in the world from time eternal in association with *ajiva* (matter). The enjoyment of this association leads to further contact, and so the cycle of birth, death and various experiences of life go on. This process could be stopped and the energies already forged destroyed, by a course of discipline leading to *nirvana* (salvation) (Jain, 1982).

Jainism perceives intrinsic equality among all selves, be they earth-bodies, water-bodies, vegetable organisms, insects, birds, animals or human beings. The attitude of equality finds expression in non-violence, both, in the domain of religious conduct, and in that of philosophical thought. All the Jain religious rites, external or internal, in every field of life, are formulated around non-violence. From the metaphysical doctrine of equality, Jainism also deduced the spiritual law of *karma,* which holds that all physical, mental, and other distinctions between self and others are only due to *karma* and not intrinsic. In the domain of philosophical thought, importance of equality gave rise to the ideology of *anekantvada* (non-absolutism) (Sanghvi, 1982).

Buddhism

According to Buddha, there are four noble truths fundamental to all the worldly life: sorrow, the cause of sorrow, the possibility of removal of sorrow and the way of removal of sorrow. According to him, the cause for the sorrow and unhappiness in the world is greed and selfishness. To be free from sorrow and unhappiness one should, therefore, be free from greed and desire. He recommended the Middle Way and the Eight-fold Path to be free from greed. The Middle Way is a way of life that avoids, both, the uncontrolled satisfaction of human desires, and the extreme forms of self-denial and self-torture. The Noble Path consists of knowledge of the truth, the intention to resist evil, saying nothing to hurt others, respecting life, morality and property, holding a job that does not injure others, striving to free one's mind of evil, controlling one's feelings and thoughts and practising proper forms of concentration (*The World Book Encyclopedia*, 1988).

Implications

Jainism and Buddhism, both, promoted equality and non-violence. These are, both, institutionalised religions, in terms of *sanghas* (order of monks), unlike Brahminism. Both influenced the governance of kings such as Chandragupta Maurya, Ashoka, Kanishka, and Harshwardhan. Buddhism is the only Indian religion which crossed over its frontiers into Asia and then became a world religion. In China, Buddhism was influenced by Taoism. This combination was called Zen when it reached Japan. Zen has no dogmas and no rituals as it is mystical.

After the death of king Harshwardhan (647 AD), chaos, confusion and anarchy prevailed in the country. The unity of his empire disappeared and small independent states sprang up. Around 700 AD is considered the end of the ancient period in India (Kundra, 1997), marked by the beginning of frequent Arab and Afghan invasions, decline of Jainism and Buddhism, and emergence of neo-Brahminism.

Spirituality

The *Upanishads* form the basis of spirituality. They provide a method of psychic development that leads us to the realisation of the ultimate truth. Spiritual experiences are supra-mental and supra-conceptual experiences. In the spiritual approach, there is a necessity to bring all the inner forces under control and regulate them in such a way that a mental and psychic harmony of being is established before thinking of the highest spiritual realisation. There is insistence upon identity between the seeking self and the object of worship. It has the objective of awakening the cosmic nature sleeping in human beings, and of unveiling their divine nature. This intuition gives a new knowledge which is not possible for reason to give. The self now becomes dislocated from its limited centre, encompasses the whole existence and finally transcends it. This experience makes life supra-ethical (Sircar, 1982).

Buddha firmly established the spiritual tradition, making it available to all. It is the notion of truth that occupies the centre in Indian spirituality. Truth need not depend on worship of

God, that is a personal God or a deity. Knowing the truth amounts to a resolution of the mystery of human existence. What it demands is an enquiry, a journey into oneself and not towards something outside of human existence – transcendent God or heaven. Search not faith, knowledge not belief, meditation not worship, freedom not heaven, are other contrasting themes which explain the difference between spirituality and religion (Agarwal, 1998).

A spiritual discourse thus, in its very nature, is secular. It considers any reference to the authority of religion as totally irrelevant to its spiritual enterprise of the search for truth. In the spiritual tradition, truth is, in principle, accessible to all in this very life, if the aspirant reaches out directly to it (Agarwal, 1998).

MEDIEVAL PERIOD

Zoroastrianism in India

Zoroaster is supposed to have lived in about 1000 BC in Persia, whose religion Zoroastrianism was the national religion of the Persian Empire, from the 3rd to the 7th century AD. His *gathas* or religious books are called the *Avestas*, of which only a fraction survives today. These books talk of a formless God as Ahura-Mazda, from whom everything emanates and in whom everything merges back. The three great commandments he recommended are good thought, good word and good deed. The first place is given to good thought, which is considered the most important instrument for the spiritual journey. Good word emphasises adherence to the truth. Good deed for others is necessary for happiness to oneself (Taraporewala, 1993).

When Iran had to face Islam, Zoroastrianism could not hold its own and was very nearly wiped out from the land of its birth. A few Zoroastrians clung to the ancient fire of Ahura-Mazda and took refuge in India in 936 AD (Taraporewala, 1993).

Islam in India

Islam originated in 7th century Arabia with the prophet Mohammed and a holy text called *Koran*. His teachings helped reform the practices of the warring tribes of Arabia and unite them into one nation (Vas, 1997). There are five main principles or pillars of Islam: (1) the affirmation that there is no God but God and Mohammed as His prophet, (2) prayer five times a day, (3) *zakat* or the giving of two and a half per cent of one's holdings as alms, (4) fasting in the month of Ramadan, during which the *Koran* was revealed, and (5) *Haj*, or pilgrimage to Mecca, where Mohammed was born, at least once in a lifetime (Marshall, 1994).

Over and above these five main duties, Muslims must abstain from gambling, drinking and eating pork. They must accept *Sharia* as, both, the system of law and rule of life, setting ethical ideals. They must remain united in eliminating all external and internal enemies of God. A Muslim must earn a living and no interest is allowed to be charged (Singhal, 1983).

Arabs had been trading with India even before the birth of Islam. Arab merchants had carried back stories of India's riches. From eighth to 11th centuries, the Arabs and Afghans invaded India and carried back treasures. India was vulnerable to these attacks at this time, as most of the small states in northern India were ruled by Rajput kings who lacked political unity. They started a practice of giving land grants, instead of salaries, to the officers who collected revenues. With the passage of time, kings did not have direct control over the revenues and became dependent on the *jagirdars* (landlords). Thus, the Rajput kingdoms were impoverished and divided into *jagirs* held by *jagirdars* (Kundra, 1997).

In the 12th century, the Turks who belonged to the 'barbarous' tribes of hilly areas, invaded India and defeated the Rajputs. They decided to set up a kingdom in India, rather than just plundering and going back. For six centuries, Muslim rulers ruled India, first Turks and then Moghuls (Vas, 1997). India was known in the ancient period as *Bharatvarsha*, the land of Bharat, a legendary emperor. The Persians called the country the land of the river Sindhu, which was pronounced as Hindu. The Muslim rulers called it *Hindustan*.

The interface of the Indian and the Muslim cultures brought assimilations in the forms of Urdu language, Kathak dance, *sitar* and *tabla* musical instruments, *ghazals* as a form of poetry, *salwar kameez* dresses, food items and so on (Vas, 1997). Islam promoted non-idol worship in India. However, the interface also drove the Muslims to a more intense life of religious austerities and inspired the Brahmins to seek more earnestly for the truths of their faith.

Born about 686 AD, Sankara, who belonged to Kerala, carried out research, writing and teaching on *Vedas* and *Upanishads*, making them once again the most important religious scriptures in India. This led to the emergence of a more organised neo-Brahminism that began to dominate society and made customs rigid and coercive, especially for women and the Dalits. The emergent problems were child marriages, female infanticide, polygamy, practice of *Sati*, untouchability, and so on. Strictly bound by the tenets of their own scriptures, the two religions had no meeting points with each other. When disunity between the two was growing, it was left to the Hindu Bhaktas and the Mohammedan Sufis to construct a bridge between the two religions (Sen, 1993).

Mysticism of Bhakti and Sufi Movements

Mysticism is the ideology common to the Bhaktas and the Sufis. According to Bose (1964), the mystics believed in the success of love where intellect fails. The spirit was free from those superstitions and rigidities, which caused stagnation among the classical Indian and Islamic schools. The mystics are, by nature, tolerant as they see a single truth in all religions (Zaehner, 1994). According to the mystical ideology, the truth or God may be known through spiritual insight, independent of the mind. The mystic ideology is unitive and transcends the subject-object duality. The mystics fostered humaneness, benevolence, charity, tenderness and love, on the basis of realisation of the supreme worth of fellow human beings.

There were two general divisions of the Bhakti traditions: *Sagun* and *Nirgun* traditions. *Sagun* means having qualities and possessing a concretised form. Mirabai, Tulsidas, Chaitanya, and Surdas, particularly, belonged to this school. If God had human form, and could be depicted through an image, 'he' could have had a life-story and could have become a subject of a sacred text; thus temples were needed to worship 'him'. This perception of God was full of sincere emotion and formed a basis for much beautiful poetry, but it consisted of premises which brought it very close to the 'official' Hindu cult (Vanina, 1996).

Kabir was the forerunner of the *Nirgun* Bhakti movement. The adherents of this Bhakti tradition followed strict monotheism and believed that God was an absolute, without any visible form or life-story, hence no temples, rituals and priests were needed to worship 'him'. Doctrines like these brought *Nirgun* Bhakti close to Sufism. Many sects of the *Nirgun* Bhakti were joined by the Muslims (Vanina, 1996).

The Sufi sect had originated in Iran. Khwaja Moinuddin Chisti was a renowned philosopher among the Sufi saints, who came to India. According to Zaehner (1994), the strictly monotheistic religions do not lend themselves to mysticism. Sufism is so radically a different form of the orthodox doctrine of Islam, as to constitute almost a separate religion. Shah (1964) noted that Sufis respect the rituals of religion insofar as these further social harmony, but broaden the religion's doctrinal basis, wherever possible, and define its myths in a higher sense.

The Bhaktas/saints/poets and Sufis strived for communal and caste harmony, for achieving harmony between the two religions and reaching religion to all the people. They rebelled against the caste hierarchy and Brahminism, child marriage, ill-treatment of widows, and other such social evils. They were not scholars who preached in temples, but were simple men and women, who belonged to various classes, castes and occupations. They went from place to place, singing hymns and using people's language and poems. In fact, the rise of the Bhakti movement led to the rise of the different regional languages. The Bhaktas rejected ritualism and unnecessary religious ceremonies, developed religious tolerance, focussed upon love and devotion to God, lived a simple life and reached out to the people. They generated a mass social consciousness that, what the priests say is not the final word on religion. However, their main aim was to save an individual soul, not improve the society. Punishment of the oppressors was entrusted to God (Vanina, 1996).

Sikhism

Guru Nanak, who was born in 1469, was greatly influenced by the teachings of Kabir and Indian Sufis. He accepted good things from, both, Hinduism and Islam. Drawing from *Nirgun* Bhakti, he preached against image worship, caste system and meaningless religious practices. His teachings are written in the *Adi Granth*. His followers are called Sikhs (Vas, 1997). Sikhs recognise a single impersonal God, reject Brahminism and acknowledge that all are equal before God (Glossary of Terms, 1998).

Relations between the Moghul rulers and Sikhs began to deteriorate in the time of Jahangir, when he executed the fifth Sikh Guru, Arjun Dev. By the time Aurangzeb had settled into power, he had initiated an anti-Sikh policy with vigour. As a result, Sikhs who had originally begun as a religious order, transformed into a powerful military body, under the leadership of the ninth Guru Teg Bahadur (Singhal, 1983).

Guru Gobind was the 10th and the last guru of the Sikhs. Under his leadership, the Sikhs became a powerful brotherhood of soldiers. They promised to keep themselves ready at all times to defend their faith and their people. They began to wear *kirpans* or *swords*. They were given new names with the title 'Singh', which means lion, added to them. When Guru Gobind Singh died, he told his people that after him there will be no guru and they must accept the *Adi Granth* as their guru. This is why the book is called *Guru Granth Sahib* (Vas, 1997).

MODERN PERIOD

Christianity in India

The church of the Christians of South India, known as the Syrian Christians, was founded by St. Thomas, one of the apostles of Jesus Christ. The earliest historical evidence of a church in South India dates from the sixth century AD. With the arrival of Vasco de Gama in 1498, the influence of the Roman Catholic Church was brought to bear upon this ancient church. Christian expansion in north India is associated with the political and commercial expansion of Europe (Abraham, 1993).

On the eve of the British conquest, India had a network of institutions which imparted religious knowledge. There was no institution of secular study. Christian missionaries started English schools, which were open to all peoples (Singhal, 1983). This education exposed the Indians to the modern ideologies of rationalism and liberalism and the values of freedom, equality and justice. However, it also imparted the attitude that India had no culture worth the name, and that Indians needed to remould themselves with the Europeans to be considered civilised (Swami Nirvedananda, 1993).

Besides the education system, the Christian missionaries exposed the Indians to a new approach to religion. Christian missionaries also started to build dispensaries and orphanages in India. They worked against illiteracy, disease and poverty, especially among the tribals and Dalits. The evangelistic purpose and the call to service, in every form, were inseparable parts of their obligations (Abraham, 1993). The missionaries attacked customs such as child marriage, polygamy, female infanticide, *Sati* and so on. They tried to show how Christianity believed in the innate equality of all human beings and how it was free from the many superstitions and the rigid ritualism that characterised popular Hinduism.

Grewal (1999) noted that the Christian missionaries began the use of the term 'Hinduism' for the Brahminical systems of religious practice. They perceived 'Hinduism' as a monolithic whole, imposing conceptual unity on a plural empirical reality. A secular identity was thus transformed into a religious identity, leading in due course to the conception of a monolithic Hindu community, although religions in India evolved independently and did not constitute a single historically evolved religion (Panikkar, 1998).

Hindu Reform Movements

Historical Context of Origin and Development

The European nation-states started trade with India after Vasco de Gama found the new sea route to India in 1498. In 1600, a small group of British merchants formed a company called the East India Company in India. After the death of Aurangzeb, the Moghul rule became weak and many independent kingdoms came up. This gave opportunity to the trading British to interfere in the affairs of these kingdoms. By 1767, the traders had become the rulers of India. The goods, that were in demand in the European markets, were purchased by the British at the lowest possible prices in India. On the other hand, they sold their goods in India at a high price, thereby earning enormous profits. To earn more and more profit from the colonial trade, they imposed various restrictions on India. The British introduced Western education in India, hoping that it would create a consumer class for English industrial products (*History of India,* 1996).

Perception of People and Social Problems

Raja Ram Mohan Roy of Bengal was the first person in the 19th century to make efforts to defend Hinduism against the criticism of Christian missionaries from outside, and the danger of it being debased by superstitions and ritualistic practices from within. He went back to the Vedic and Upanishadic thought for the purpose. The religious and social reform activities, that he began, took root and set the pattern for similar activities in other parts of the country. Most of the reformers of the 19th century were educated elite who had been influenced by the Western liberal thought. They perceived societal problems to have roots in religion. The upper caste reformers' argument was essentially to the effect that their religion was fundamentally right and what was required was only the shedding of the extraneous impurities that had entered into the social life of the people. Revival of Hinduism, synthesis of religious faiths and modernisation were, therefore, considered necessary (Gore, 1965).

Ideals, Rationale and Goals for Social Change

Values such as rationalism, individualism, humanism embedded in European society during the Renaissance period, began to take roots in India as well. Besides these values, the reformers were led by the liberal ideals of democracy and democratic procedures in political and social organisation, equality, value of education, science and knowledge and the need for rationality in public life (Gore, 1966).

Approach to Social Change

Raja Ram Mohan Roy established Brahmo Samaj in 1828 in Bengal. It worked for the emancipation of women and abolition of the caste system. Prarthna Samaj in Bombay was its offshoot. Arya Samaj was established by Dayanand Saraswati, in 1875, in the North. It worked to abolish the caste system, deny the monopoly of the Brahmins over the *Vedas*, and liberate women from a number of disabilities. Spread of education was a remarkable feature of the philanthropic activities of Arya Samaj. The Theosophical Society, that was set up in New York, in 1825, also contributed substantially to revive the faith of Indians in their ideologies (Swami Nirvedananda, 1993).

Sri Ramakrishna Paramhans (1834-86) preached selfless devotion to God and sought self-realisation. He preached the old religion of India founded on the *Vedas* and the *Upanishads* and systematised in later commentaries. His dynamic disciple, Swami Vivekanand (1863-1902) preached the teachings of his guru. While Ramakrishna was a mystic depending upon intuition and vision, Vivekanand was an intellectual, relying mainly upon reason. He interpreted Indian thought impressively to Western peoples and provided a bridge between East and West. He founded the Ramakrishna Mission at Belur, in 1897, which adopted a comprehensive programme of social services. It has developed into a worldwide organisation today (Singhal, 1983).

Apart from seeking a change in attitudes or values through a process of community education, a good deal of the reformist's attention was devoted to seeking new legislation which would either consolidate the changes already effected or help in bringing them about. Besides religious revival and translation of scriptures, setting up schools and encouraging education, setting up hospitals, care of the disabled, orphanages, homes for widows, relief for the poor, and so on, were some of the other activities undertaken by the reformers. Full-time functionaries were necessary for these activities, in the form of voluntary workers. Simplicity in personal life, self-example and signing pledges, were some of the approaches they used (Gore, 1966).

Critique and Implications

In spite of reforms in legislation, the orthodox masses under the traditional lead of Brahmins and Pundits, continued their old socio-religious practices (Swami Nirvedananda, 1993). As Gore (1987) noted, a reformist activity which is heavily based on law, often becomes ineffective because a change in law which is not supported by a change in popular attitudes and in social context, cannot achieve its goal.

The reformers strengthened the construct of Hinduism, which led to increase in the Hindu hegemony (Grewal, 1999). The religion of the Brahmins became the framework for the construction of Hinduism. The bunching together of all the indigenous sects and labelling them as Hindus was alien to the earlier tradition where religious identity was by sect and the term Hindu was not used. This led to the notion of majority and minority communities based on religion, preventing the possibility of other kinds of classification and identities (Thapar, 1998). The reformers were against untouchability but not against the caste system. They, therefore, could not deal with caste persecution. The Dalits started getting converted to Christianity. The problems of the poor and the rural were also neglected.

In the 1880s, a debate arose on whether social reform should precede political reform or vice versa. The orthodox opposition argued that the foreign rule alone was responsible for all the ills; that the social reformers were playing into the hands of the foreign rulers who would welcome the excuse that people must remove the social injustices before they could advance politically. Lokmanya Tilak led the opposition to the social reform movement, which according to him, would divide the mass support essential for the nationalist cause.

Dalit* and Labour Movements

The Brahmin-dominated caste system was critiqued by Jainism and Buddhism, which welcomed peoples across castes to join them. During the Muslim rule, many 'untouchables' and 'low' caste people embraced Islam, partly to avoid persecution and partly in search of better status and fortunes. It was during the British rule that the Dalit movement could have begun. Teltumbde (1998) notes that the British did many good things for the Dalits. They introduced a modern legal system which disowned caste as a basis for law, and opened up educational and employment opportunities for them in European families, mills and factories, railways and shipping, and the army. The colonial state thus became the basic enabler and catalyst of the Dalit movement.

Jotiba Phule, a *Shudra*, by caste, formulated the theory of exploitation by the Aryans of an originally prosperous and egalitarian society in India. He rejected the *Vedas* and proposed an egalitarian religious alternative, which he called, Sarvajanik Satya Dharma. He founded the Satyashodhak Samaj in 1875, which organised the non-Brahmins, uniting *Shudras* and the

---

* Dalit literally means the oppressed. This term came into wide usage with the formation of Dalit Panthers in the early 1970s. According to Dalit Panthers, all exploited sections of society: workers, women, scheduled castes, and tribes are Dalit. The term has come to be used more for the latter two groups, replacing earlier terms such as Shudra and Harijan (Glossary of Terms, 1998).

Atishudras, in order to propound rationality, give up Brahmin priests for rituals, and educate children (Omvedt, 1996).

In the early 19th century, several Dalit movements started in different parts of India. The Satnami movement, in Madhya Pradesh, was led by Ghasi Das, a *chamar*, who promoted the worship of God by the name Satnami. The Adi-Dharma movement, in Punjab, identified Dalits as a separate cultural entity and protested against their present identity as untouchables under the Hindu fold. The Ezhavas movements, in Kerala, felt that Hinduism by itself was not bad, only the practice of untouchability was bad. Around the early 20th century, the Nadar movement in Tamil Nadu, strove to elevate the Dalits from the low position in the caste hierarchy, to get access to all those rituals and other religious services which were denied to them under the Hindu fold. The Nadars also concentrated on enhancing their economic and political status and succeeded in obtaining a higher status in the caste hierarchy (Ramaiah, 1998).

The decade of the 1920s saw the emergence of a vigorous Dalit movement, in Bombay Presidency, under the leadership of Dr. Babasaheb Ambedkar. When he protested against Brahminism, he spoke against all caste Hindus, emphasising the interest of the untouchables. He advised and promoted conversion to Buddhism. He established the All India Scheduled Caste Federation in 1942, which was replaced by the Republic Party of India (RPI) in 1957, which is popular only in Maharashtra today (Ramaiah, 1998). He brought a constitutional ban on untouchability and reservation for Dalits and tribals in education, employment and political participation.

The Indian peasants were the worst sufferers of the exploitative economic policy of the British, who extended protection to the *zamindars* (landlords) and moneylenders. In the latter half of the 19th century, the peasants rose in revolt a number of times, especially in Bengal and Maharashtra. In 1918, the Kisan Sabha was established in Uttar Pradesh. After the First World War, with industrialisation, there emerged a large working class in India. Influenced by the Marxist ideology, the Communist Party was established in India in 1925 (*History of India,* 1996).

In the 1920s and the 1930s, the Dalit activists, peasants and workers of the time confronted the formulation of a radical class ideology by the New Left intelligentsia. The latter avoided the recognition of caste and stressed a mechanical class framework that sought to override traditional identities rather than reinterpret them. Being mainly from the middle class and upper castes, they regarded the caste question as an unimportant issue, which would automatically disappear when revolution took place (Teltumbde, 1998). On the other hand, the open anti-state stance of the communists, did not find favour with the Dalits. The broad movement of the oppressed in the 1930s was split into a class movement and a caste movement as there was no development of an integrated ideology. As a result, the anti-caste movement lost its sharpness (Omvedt, 1994).

Under the hegemony of the nationalist movement, the leadership of Congress strove to take over the agendas of several subaltern movements. They believed that the main problem was the oppressed Indian nationality and imperialism. Like the Marxists, most nationalists saw the Dalit movement as basically divisive and dangerously pro-British (Omvedt, 1994).

Gandhian Ideology and Sarvodaya Movement

Gandhiji, leader of the freedom movement in the first half of the 20th century, was concerned about the need for change in social, religious, economic as well as political structures that victimise people, especially the Dalits, women, rural, the tribal, and labourers. The values that he insisted among his followers were, non-violence, truth, non-stealing, personal restraint, non-accumulation, *shramdan* (bodily labour), non-attachment to pleasures of the palate, elimination of all fears, religious tolerance, *swadeshi* and removal of untouchability. For Gandhiji, it was necessary that the stated objectives, as also the means utilised for their achievement, be socially justifiable (Gore, 1987).

Gandhiji suggested non-cooperation in the operation of an unjust system and self-suffering in the assertion of a cherished social value -- *satyagraha* (the force of truth) -- as the way to attain the desired objective. The ideology of *satyagraha* empowers the common people to fight injustice. It increases their moral strength and makes them fearless. They face the consequences of their opposition with equanimity and it is this suffering that awakens the conscience of the oppressor. The *satyagrahis* do not harbour any ill-feelings and fear, but have love and compassion towards the oppressor. This makes the oppressor realise the truth and the truth triumphs (*Imperialism and Indian Freedom Struggle,* 1998). According to him, *ahimsa* (non-violence) was the only way for *satyagraha* as violent methods are bound to fail in the long run.

Gandhiji was troubled with large institutions that distanced themselves from the people. In particular, he believed that large corporate industries and centralised governments were unable to address the spiritual and social development needs of populations, especially rural populations. In response to corporate approaches that tended towards social control, he recommended locally controlled forms of organisation. Material simplicity was an important principle for Gandhiji. This principle advocates moderation in consumption – living a full life without taking unnecessary material things. He also included some corollary principles such as non-attachment, non-stealing and trusteeship. He offered trusteeship as a solution for those who had already accumulated more than they needed. He also advocated that those with surplus wealth should voluntarily share with those in need (Walz and Ritchie, 2000).

For Gandhiji, self-governance was more important than freedom from the British. His notion of rural development was constructing *gram swarajya* (self-supporting, self-governing, and self-reliant village communities), which would replace *rajniti* (ruler's policy) by *lokniti* (people's policy), abolish caste and class differences and so on. He also made a suggestion that the Congress party may be disbanded and converted into a movement for social reconstruction, which was rejected (Sethi, 1989).

Gandhiji believed that voluntary action was the only path to India's development. The Sarvodaya (well-being of all) movement brought dignity and self-respect to the common person. This movement had prepared the ground to make it seem natural that India should accept a constitution which embodies the goal of social justice and social equality (Gore, 1966). In 1951, Vinoba Bhave gave shape to the idea of *Bhoodan* (land gift). In 1952, *Bhoodan* paved the way for *Gramdan* (village gift). In 1963, *Gramdan*, *Khadi* and *Shanti Sena* (peace force) were integrated as a triple programme under the Sarvodaya movement.

Gandhiji's vision of Sarvodaya was a casteless and classless society. The Sarvodaya movement reached its peak in the early 1970s. In 1971, Jayaprakash Narayan started a campaign against Mrs. Indira Gandhi's government, which reached its peak during the Emergency (1975-77). The movement helped the Janata Party to win the 1977 elections and the Janata rule helped to promote the Sarvodaya movement. The government's control on the voluntary sector began to increase when the Janata Party went out of power in 1980 and the Congress Party was re-elected. The new government appointed a major commission of inquiry, the Kudal Commission, in retaliation against the support given to Jayaprakash by the Sarvodaya organisations. The Commission made allegations about missing funds against 945 Gandhian organisations. The

Commission was dissolved in 1986-87, when a younger group of voluntary organisation officials was successful in its campaign to end it (Sen, 1998).

Nationalism

Throughout history, people have been attached to their native soil, to the traditions of their parents, and to established territorial authorities; but it was not until the end of the 18th century that nationalism began to be one of the great single determining factors of modern history. Nationalism as a people's sense of belonging together as a nation, emerged along with the development of the nation-states. It is an ideology based on the premise that the individual's loyalty and devotion to the nation-state surpass other individual or group interests. Nationalism translated into world politics, implies the identification of the state or nation with the people or at least the desirability of determining the extent of the state according to ethnographic principles. Only in the age of nationalism, the principle was generally recognised that each nationality should form a state – its state – and that the state should include all members of that nationality (*Encyclopaedia Britannica*, 2001). Tagore (1950) noted that a nation, in the sense of the political and economic union of a people, is that aspect which a whole population assumes when organised for a mechanical purpose.

The 19th century has been called the age of nationalism in Europe, while the 20th century has witnessed the rise and struggle of powerful national movements throughout Asia and Africa (*Encyclopaedia Brittanica*, 2001). According to Ram (1999), the initial nationalism that emerged in India during the British rule, was not anti-British. It was this nationalism that led to the different reform movements, new associations and unions of economic, social and political nature on the Western pattern. In fact, the Indian intellectuals believed in the view held by the British that the 18th century was a 'Dark Age' for India, comprising of anarchy, intellectual stagnation and cultural backwardness. They viewed the British rule as a well-established state system, which was leading India to the path of political and economic modernisation. This made them develop an idealised view of the state (Panikkar, 1995).

By the early 1920s, a semblance of ambivalence towards the idea of a monocultural nation-state and towards nationalism appeared in the Indian freedom movement, notably among Gandhiji, Dr. Ambedkar and Rabindranath Tagore. While they continued to view an anti-imperialist stand as being an almost sacred responsibility, they refused to accept the Western idea of nationalism as being the inevitable universal of the times. They did not want the idea of the Indian nation to supersede that of the Indian civilisation, where the actual ways of life of Indians would be assessed solely in terms of the needs of an imaginary nation-state called India (Nandy, 1994).

Rabindranath Tagore (1950) noted that under the British rule, for the first time India had to deal not with kings, but with a nation – "we, who were no nation ourselves". According to him, nation as a political and economic union of people becomes all-powerful, it is at the cost of the harmony of the higher social life. It is the organised self-interest of a whole people, where it is least human and least spiritual. Under the influence of nationalism, the whole people can carry out its systematic programme of the most virulent self-seeking without being the least aware of its moral perversion. It is assuming gigantic proportions and power, causing the upset of people's moral balance, and obscuring their human side under the shadow of a soul-less organisation.

According to Tagore (1950), the economic and political organisation of the nation comprises of law and order, military organisation, magisterial offices, the police, the Criminal Investigation Department, and the secret spy system, rendering people powerless. It gives them freedom only of the material world. This organisation incessantly heaps up the insistence of the population on becoming strong and efficient. Thereby people's power of sacrifice is diverted from their ultimate object, which is moral, to the maintenance of the organisation, which is mechanical. Thus, people's mental and material power far outgrows their moral strength.

The Dalit movement discussed the premise of the mainstream nationalist movement that India was a nation, as it is a caste-based society (Teltumbde, 2000). Hinduism and nationalism emerged around the same time, under the British rule, which led to equating Hinduism with nationalism, (Omvedt, 1996). Communal politics in India began as a response to the development of the nationalist movement. This politics projects the belief that all people belonging to one religion have common economic, social and political interests and that these interests are contrary to those of the ones belonging to other religions (Ram, 1998).

Ideology of the Indian Constitution

Historical Context of Origin and Development

The Constitution of India was adopted, in 1949 and put into force in 1950. It resolved India into a sovereign socialist secular democratic republic. By sovereign is meant that India is free to follow its policies without any foreign interference. By socialist is meant that India aims at economic and social equality. By secular is meant that India has no official religion and it would not discriminate against any religion. By democratic is meant that people can choose their government by votes. By republic is meant that the head of India is an elected person who holds the office for a definite period. It aims to secure its citizens justice (social, economic and political), liberty (of thought, expression, belief, faith and worship), equality (of status and opportunity) and fraternity (assuring the dignity of the individual and unity and integrity of the nation).

Inspired by the Universal Declaration of Human Rights, Part III of the constitution comprises of the Fundamental Rights that provide the capitalistic orientation and Part IV of the Constitution comprises of the Directive Principles of State Policy, that provide the socialist orientation. Part III is justiciable, whereas, Part IV is not justiciable. Part IV A lists the Fundamental Duties that mainly promote nationalism.

Ideals, Rationale and Goals for Social Change

Fundamental Rights

1. Right to Equality includes the following rights:
   - Equality before law
   - Prohibition of discrimination
   - Equality of opportunities in matters of public employment. This will not prevent the state from making special provisions for women, children, scheduled castes and scheduled tribes
   - Abolition of untouchability and titles.
2. Right to Freedom includes the following rights:
   - Freedom of speech and expression
   - Peaceful assembly and form associations or unions
   - Move freely in India, reside anywhere, hold or acquire property
   - Practice any profession. Laws can be enacted for security, public order, decency or morality, or in relation to contempt of court or defamation.
3. Right against Exploitation includes the following rights:
   - Prohibition of traffic in human beings and forced and child labour.

4. Right to Freedom of Religion
5. Cultural and Educational Rights include the following rights:
   — Protection of minority culture.
   — Rights of minorities to establish and administer educational institutions.
6. Right to Constitutional Remedies

Directive Principles of State Policy

These principles are fundamental in the governance of the country. It is the duty of the state to apply these principles in making laws, in order to secure a social order for the promotion of welfare of the people. In such a social order, social, economic and political justice shall inform all the institutions of the national life. The following principles are included in this document:

— Equality between men and women.

— Protection of children and youth from neglect and abuse.

— Organisation of village *panchayats*.

— Right to work, to education and to public assistance in case of unemployment, old age, sickness and disablement. Provision of just and humane conditions for work and maternity relief.

— Uniform civil code for citizens.

— Free and compulsory education for children.

— Promotion of educational and economic interests of scheduled castes, scheduled tribes and other weaker sections.

— Provision to raise the level of nutrition, standard of living, and improved public health.

Conversion of Directive Principles into Fundamental Rights

The Directive Principles which were declared unforceable but fundamental to the governance of the country have been gradually converted into Fundamental Rights, since the 1980s. The new rights are created by the Supreme Court of India, through its corpus of activist jurisprudence. These are rights to dignity, livelihood, compensation and rehabilitation for injuries done or caused by state agents or agencies, speedy trial, health, education, gender equality and environment (Baxi, 1998).

Fundamental Duties

Part IV A of the Constitution lists the following fundamental duties:

(a) to abide by the Constitution and respect its ideals and institutions, the National Flag and the National Anthem;

(b) to cherish and follow the noble ideals which inspired our national struggle for freedom;

(c) to uphold and protect the sovereignty, unity and integrity of India;

(d) to defend the country and render national service when called upon to do so;

(e) to promote harmony and the spirit of common brotherhood amongst all the people of India transcending religious, linguistic and regional or sectional diversities; to renounce practices derogatory to the dignity of women;

(f) to value and preserve the rich heritage of our composite culture;

(g) to protect and improve the natural environment including forests, lakes, rivers and wild-life, and to have compassion for living creatures;

(h) to develop the scientific temper, humanism and the spirit of inquiry and reform;

(i) to safeguard public property and to abjure violence; and

(j) to strive towards excellence in all spheres of individual and collective activity so that the nation constantly rises to higher levels of endeavour and achievement.

Critique and Implications

Because the Fundamental Rights are the needs of the haves and justiciable, they have dominated the governance and not the Directive Principles.

The Ministry of Welfare, now called the Ministry of Social Justice and Empowerment, is the main infrastructure to deal with the marginalised groups such as the scheduled castes and tribes, children, disabled, elderly and women. It functions devoid of the ethos of the Directive Principles of securing a just social order, as it lays down "schemes" that delivers services to the marginalised people as beneficiaries, which does not help to change the unjust social order. The Government responds to human rights issues of the marginalised only when the United Nations formulates specific conventions which are to be ratified by and are then legally binding on the member countries.

Ideology of Voluntary Organisations

The voluntary political freedom movement was imbued with a larger vision of transforming state and society before independence. After independence, the transforming functions became the sole prerogative of the state and political parties. The voluntary organisations during the freedom movement did not depend on the state for resources and directions. The resources were raised through donations or people's contributions. After independence, these started relying upon the official system for funds, patronage and legitimacy and essentially became a 'delivery system' for providing relief and succour to affected populations (Sethi, 1989). What remained of these organisations was an attitude of compassion without questioning why the victim groups become and remain so (Baxi, 1997).

Summary Chart 5

Indian Ideologies in their Historical and Societal Context and Implications

Historical Stage	*Societal Context*	*Ideologies*	*Implications*
Ancient Period: Up to 7th century	Agricultural and horticultural society, Indus valley civilisation Aryan invasion Caste system	Vedic ideology	Promotion of Dharma (duties) and Dana (charity) Development of Brahminism
		Jain and Buddh ideologies	Promotion of equality, non-violence and the middle way
		Spirituality	Promotion of secularism
Medieval Period: 8th to 16th centuries	Trade with Arabs, Turk and Moghul rule	Zoroastrianism and Islam in India	Plurality of religions in India Promoted non-idol worship Revival of Brahminism
		Mysticism of Bhakti and Sufi movements Sikhism	Promotion of communal harmony, religion accessible for all
Modern Period: 17th century to 1950s	Trade with Europeans, British rule, Freedom movement Independence	Christianity in India, Hindu reform movements	Introduction of modern ideologies, strengthening of Hinduism, promotion of philanthropy
		Dalit and labour movements	Promotion of mass social consciousness

Contd...

Contd...

Historical Stage	*Societal Context*	*Ideologies*	*Implications*
Medieval Period: 8th to 16th centuries		Gandhian ideology and Sarvoday movement	Promotion of a holistic approach to social change
		Nationalism	Homogenisation of society Centralisation of governance Beginning of communal politics
		Ideology of the Indian Constitution	Promotion of secularism Fundamental Rights of equality and freedom more important than Directive Principles of State Policy of a just social order
		Ideology of voluntary organisations	From social change to service delivery system

Module 4

Indian History of Ideologies of Social Work Profession

TEACHER/LEARNER OBJECTIVES

The module on 'Indian History of Ideologies of Social Work Profession' may have the following teacher/learner objectives:

1. Analyse the influence of the Western ideology of professional social work and the Indian ideologies for social change on ideologies of social work profession in India.
2. Examine the professionalisation of the normative and the cognitive attributes of social work in India.

BEGINNING OF SOCIAL WORK EDUCATION

Gopal Krishna Gokhale founded the Servants of India Society, in 1905, which was probably the first major organisation in the field of social work which did not have a religious basis. He insisted on a scholarly study of the problems for which they sought solutions. He thus paved the way for a rational and scientific (if not professional) approach to the solution of social problems (Gore, 1965). Another precursor to professional social work was the Social Service League in Bombay which started a training class, in 1924, to train the voluntary cadre for social development. They offered a series of lectures on social subjects and introduced the students to the various social work activities being carried out in the city, for voluntary unpaid services. Apart from that, social work in India had been, in large measure, a matter of apprentice training. The young social worker learned from being associated with an older worker, or even more commonly, by engaging in work and acquiring a technique and proficiency through experience (Manshardt, 1967).

The first professional school of social work, Sir Dorabji Tata Graduate School of Social Work was set up in Bombay by Sir Dorabji Tata Trust, in 1936, with an American missionary, Sir Clifford Manshardt, as its first director. This school is now known as the Tata Institute of Social Sciences (TISS). Sir Manshardt had obtained his social work experience in a settlement house in Chicago. He had founded a settlement house called the Nagpada Neighbourhood House in Bombay. He was convinced that in order to raise the standard of social work in India appreciably, a permanent school of social work was needed, to engage in a continuous study of Indian social problems and to offer training for social work at the post-graduate level. This school was initiated in the Nagpada Neighbourhood House. To start the school, the bibliography was prepared by the University of Chicago library and curriculum planning was drawn from American and British schools of social work (Manshardt, 1967). Thus started the legacy of American professional social work in India.

PROFESSIONALISATION OF SOCIAL WORK

Normative Attributes

Ideologies

The ideologies of professional social work in India have had to face some similarities and some contradictions, with reference to the Indian ideologies, based in its social ethos, religions and indigenous social movements. The Indian society is structured by families and communities, whereas, the Western social work approach is individualistic. The Indian religions emphasise duties, whereas, the Western liberalism emphasise freedom as the goal. While the Indian ideologies are holistic and wisdom-oriented, the American professional ideology is analytical and scientism-oriented. The ideology of Indian social work profession today seems to have evolved as a combination of focus on individuals, families and communities, with the goals of achieving freedom balanced by duties, and valuing scientism as well as wisdom, using the Western theories and techniques, in an eclectic manner.

In India, the term 'social work' is generally used to include almost any activity which is intended to help, restore, or promote some aspects of the physical, economic and social well-being of individuals and groups (Nagpaul, 1988). Gore (1966) noted the following difficulties in mutual understanding between professional social work and the indigenous Indian approaches: For most professionals, their work was also a source of earning their livelihood. Although they may be dedicated to their work, in the Indian tradition, there is an assumption that dedication can be established only by not drawing a salary for the work that one does. Professional social workers, on the other hand, do not grant that dedication to work is inconsistent with a desire to improve one's salary. Another traditional assumption about social work is that social workers must live a simple life, which the professional social workers may not think necessary, although their salaries are generally not high. Professional social work has, therefore, not received full acceptance in India.

Attempts at indigenisation of social work profession in India, with reference to application of Hindu religious scriptures to philanthropy, were somewhat made by Banerjee (1972). She tried to show the continuity between traditional Indian values and the values of professional social work (Gore, 1972).

The importing of social work profession took place in India at the time when Mahatma Gandhi was mobilising people for social reconstruction. Later known as the Sarvoday movement, this approach was based on the recognition of the need for change in social, religious, economic and political structures that victimise the weaker population, namely Dalits, women, rural people, tribals, labourers and so on. The interface between professional social workers and Gandhian workers, at the time of initiation of professional social work and at a later stage, was marginal.

Efforts were made to apply Gandhian philosophies to social work by Yasas in 1964. In the same year, an attempt was made to bring together the professional social workers and Gandhian constructive workers, for the first time, in order to evolve an integrated ideology of social work for India. A working group, entitled 'Concepts, Contents and Approaches of Professional Social Work and Gandhian Constructive Work', was appointed by the Gandhian Institute of Studies. The book, *Towards a Philosophy of Social Work in India,* edited by Sugata Dasgupta, in 1967, contains the full report of the group as well as a number of original articles by its members and the report of a conference. Both the groups emphasised personal and social change. However, the programme of constructive work had a distinct political bias whereas social work was too apolitical, too professional and too limited in its concerns. The former saw the problem in its entirety and sought to remove it from the roots. The latter has been more remedial in orientation. Both the groups felt enriched by the exercise. The constructive workers accepted the need for a superstructure of a scientific system and sophistication of its tools of working with people. Professional social workers recognised that social work should not confine itself to ameliorative work, but should aim towards social action designed to remedy the roots of social malaise and to change the social order (Dasgupta, 1967). However, these efforts at integration, were countered by the UGC-sponsored First Review of Social Work Education, as given below.

In 1965, the first report on social work education, called *Social Work Education in Indian Universities*, was published, which was welfare-oriented. This report stated that,

> Now that the main aims of social reforms have been achieved, the task of the social worker has taken a different form...he has to look after the needs of children in orphanages, rehabilitate unmarried mothers and save children from the stigma of illegitimacy...Today the field of social work coalesces more or less with the field of social workers in the West. Now that the social worker has ceased to be the social reformer in the old sense, it has become possible to benefit from the experience of social work training institutions in other countries.

In 1966, a seminar was organised by the Association of Schools of Social Work in India (ASSWI) on the role of social work profession in social reconstruction. Social action was conceived at this seminar as a method of social work (Siddiqui, 1997). The ASSWI put together the papers presented at the seminar organised on Social Development Aspects of Social Education in 1973. The seminar called for a shift in emphasis of social work education from a remedial-rehabilitative approach to a preventive-developmental approach.

The second report on social work education, called *Review of Social Work Education in India,* was published in 1980, which was development-oriented. It differentiated the need for social work in India as against that in the US. While the main concern in the US was to provide social services to residual groups who are outside the mainstream of national life, the major problems in India is to assist the majority of the population and not a peripheral group. In fact, the report identified the global need to emphasise the teaching of social action, social policy and social administration. The scope of social work practice was vigorously debated in the 1980s. The decade produced three major works on social action: *Social Work and Social Action* (Siddiqui, 1984), *Social Action through Law* (Gandhi, 1985) and a chapter on Social Action in the *Encyclopaedia of Social Work in India* (Dasgupta, 1987).

Thus, the ideologies of Indian professional social work seem to have developed as a combination of modern professional values, values from Indian religions and social ideologies and values of Gandhian Sarvoday movement. The Western urban middle class paradigm with which the profession began, has been functional in terms of education infrastructure, job market and so on. As a result, social work professionals have an ambivalent approach towards developmental issues.

Professional Associations in Social Work

The idea of establishing professional associations was first mooted by J.M. Kumarappa, the first Indian Director of TISS, in 1961, at the annual meeting of the Indian Conference of Social Work (now known as the Indian Council of Social Welfare, established in 1947). With this, the ASSWI was initiated the same year. During the decade of 1975 to 1984, ASSWI published five books, based on seminars that it had organised on different aspects of social work education and practice.

The Indian Association of Alumni of Schools of Social Work, later known as the Indian Association of Trained Social Workers (IATSW), was established in 1963. The IATSW made representations to various Central and State Pay Commissions for higher salary scales for social workers and before the Union and State Public Service Commissions to earmark certain posts for social workers, but without much success. It received grants from the Indian Council of Social Science Research to publish a journal called *Social Work Forum*. Some efforts were made by ASSWI, in collaboration with IATSW, to define and promote minimum standards of social work education. In spite of these achievements and successes, the interest of members in this association gradually dwindled and due to internecine conflict among the members of the managing committee, the organisation went into non-existence in 1981, and could not be revived despite efforts by some professionals (Nanavatty, 1997).

Different types of social work professional associations in India and their counterparts at the Asia-Pacific and international levels are listed below:

Associations of Social Welfare Voluntary Organisations

1. International Conference of Social Welfare (ICSW)
2. Asia-Pacific Branch of ICSW
3. Indian Council of Social Welfare (ICSW)
4. ICSW State Branches

Associations of Schools of Social Work

1. International Association of Schools of Social Work (IASSW)
2. Asia-Pacific Association for Social Work Education (APASWE, established in 1971 in Bombay)

3. Association of Schools of Social Work in India (ASSWI)

Associations of Social Work Practitioners

1. International Federation of Social Workers (IFSW)
2. Asia-Pacific Branch of IFSW
3. Indian Association of Trained Social Workers (IATSW)
4. Indian Society of Professional Social Work has been recently initiated in Bangalore
5. Bombay Association of Trained Social Workers (BATSW)

Cognitive Attributes

Social Work Education

In 1950, an Advisory Board on Social Welfare, set up by the Ministry of Education, prepared a uniform syllabus for a two year social welfare course at the postgraduate level. The Department of Social Work of Lucknow University started the first undergraduate and the first PhD. programmes in social work, in 1960. At the time of the Second Review of Social Work Education (UGC, 1980), there were 34 institutions of social work education in India. Today there are 125 such institutions, only 31 of which are members of ASSWI. Moreover, there is a serious imbalance in their regional distribution. Almost half the schools are situated in the West, Maharashtra having as many as 54 schools. South has the second-largest concentration of institutions of social work education, with a total of 43. While the Northern states, together with Madhya Pradesh, have a total of 16 institutions, the Eastern region has only six institutions in all.

Table 1
Regional Distribution of Institutions for Social Work Education

Region and State	*Number of Institutions*
South	
Andhra Pradesh	8
Karnataka	13
Kerala	4
Tamil Nadu	17
Pondicherry	1
Total in the South	43
North & Centre	
Bihar	1
Delhi	4
Haryana	2
Madhya Pradesh	3
Punjab	1
Uttar Pradesh	5
Total in the North & Centre	16
West	
Gujarat	4
Maharashtra	54
Rajasthan	2
Total in the West	60
East	
Assam	1
Mizoram	1
Orissa	2
West Bengal	2
Total in the East	6
Total in India	125

The following table shows that of the 117 institutions about which information on the academic programmes is available, most of them (87.2%) offer a master's degree programme and less than half (45.3%) offer a bachelor's degree programme in social work. Desai (1985) noted that a country such as India cannot afford the luxury of proliferating the master's and doctoral degree programmes, nor should one have to teach the basics of the front-line tasks at the master's level.

Table 2

Distributions of Institutions by Academic Programmes in Social Work

Academic Programmes in Social Work	*Number of Institutions*
Bachelor's	53 (45.3.%)
Master's	102 (87.2.%)
M.Phil.	20 (17.1%)
Doctoral	34 (29.1%)
Total on which information is available	117 (100.0%)
No information	8
Total	125

Besides the two review reports on social work education, the UGC sponsored the *Report of the Curriculum Development Centre in Social Work Education* published, in 1990. In 1999, the Third Review Committee for Social Work Education was set up. In 2001, the UGC published a model curriculum for social work education.

Desai (1991) has done the following review of setting up of social work specialisations in India. TISS was the first school of social work to start specialisations, models of which were followed by other schools. Government policies and programmes and the influence of American social work education seem to be the two main factors that led to the development of specialisations. This resulted in welfare and clinical orientation in social work in India. The specialisations of TISS developed across social work fields, methods and functions.

With rapid industrialisation in the country the government and industrial concerns felt the need for special training in labour welfare administration and personnel management. The Factory Act of 1948 made it compulsory for factories employing more than 500 workers to appoint labour welfare officers. The industrial concerns and government departments had pressed the Institute to train personnel in the field since its inception. In 1948, the new specialisation in industrial relations and personnel management was started.

In the same year, 1948, specialised training in medical and psychiatric social work was also started. The report of the Health Survey and Development Committee (under the chairmanship of Sir Joseph Bhore), published in 1946, had stressed the need for setting up social service departments in hospitals and the necessity of utilising psychiatric social workers in the treatment of mental illness. The Bhore Committee also recommended TISS as an institution able to offer training in this new field of social service.

The specialisations in family and child welfare and public welfare administration were introduced in 1949. Because the field of public welfare was growing in importance at that time, a demand for suitably qualified workers was anticipated. This specialisation on public welfare administration, however, was dropped after two years.

Increased demands were made by the prison departments of provincial governments, as well as private agencies interested in the treatment of offenders and prevention of crime, for specialised training to be offered for personnel interested in prison work and juvenile courts. In response to the demand, the specialisation in criminology and correctional administration was planned in 1952.

The earlier specialisations at the Institute were built around casework as the method, and group work and community organisation were introduced together as a separate specialisation in 1952. This specialisation seems to mark a shift from reliance on American models and expertise to response to

India's needs. It was started in response to the growing interest shown in community development projects, by the central and state governments. Similarly, it was felt that there was a need for trained research workers in educational institutions, government departments, businesses and social service agencies. The Institute organised a specialisation in social research, also in 1952.

A major change that took place in 1967 was that the TISS social work specialisation in labour welfare and industrial relations became an independent degree programme, called MA in personnel management and labour welfare. Such a separation was considered necessary as personnel management with emphasis on management, administration and labour law, was growing as a profession distinct from social work. In the year 1975-76, the programme title changed from personnel management and labour welfare to its original title, personnel management and industrial relations. However, many other institutions of social work education have continued offering labour welfare/personnel management/industrial relations as a social work specialisation. In a survey of 27 institutions of social work education in India, labour welfare and personnel management was found to be the most popular specialisation as 19 institutions listed it as a social work specialisation (UGC, 1980). The same survey noted that several institutions taught only labour welfare and, at best, one other specialisation. The reason given for this is that students' interests are in the specialisations that carry greater salaries and benefits.

The First Review Committee of Social Work Education in India set up by the UGC, in 1965, was in favour of specialisation. But the Second Review Committee of UGC (1980) observed that the prevailing situation of social work in India did not favour social work specialisations. They found through a survey that some institutions of social work education included certain specialisations in their syllabi but did not really offer them. The main reasons they gave were lack of suitable staff, lack of student response and lack of employment opportunities. Thus it seems that institutions of social work education aim at offering specialisations without giving consideration to regional relevance, job opportunities and availability of qualified staff.

Social Work Research and Knowledge

Social work research and knowledge are defined by Desai (1997) as research and knowledge on various aspects of social work profession. A profession has an origin and a history of development, an ideology, values and a code of ethics, depending upon the welfare or developmental orientation of the profession. In social work, the expected methods of intervention are work with individuals, families, groups and communities, integrated social work practice, and social action. A system of research and knowledge-building and a system of education and training are essential for professionalisation. Curriculum, students, and educators are different components of an education system. Field instruction is an important element of social work education. A situation of employment and humanpower, professional associations and international and cross-cultural comparisons are other aspects of any profession. Thus defined, it may include literature developed by an author outside of the profession. On the other hand, literature developed on any social phenomenon by a social work professional, which does not draw any link with the profession, may not be considered social work literature.

Although the terms 'literature' and 'knowledge' are used synonymously, there is a need to clarify the difference between the two. Literature can be considered knowledge only when it is cumulatively organised to link new literature to previous ones and to theories. This linkage could be in the form of application, adaptation, elaboration or critique. Social work knowledge could also include linking social work practice wisdom with social science/work research/theories or drawing implications of social science/work research and theories for practice, towards development of praxis.

According to Desai, in 1997, India had published 63 books on social work profession and two editions of the *Social Work Encyclopaedia in India*. In the same year, institutions of social work education in India were publishing three journals in social work. Some milestones in development of social work literature are listed below.

Year	*Milestone*
1940	*The Indian Journal of Social Work* was started by TISS.
1949	The first book on social work, called *Students and Social Work, was published, by TISS.*
1958	The journal *International Social Work* was started by the International Conference of Social Work and International Association of Schools of Social Work, with a base in Bombay.
1962	The *Lucknow University Journal of Social Work* was started by the Department of Social Work of Lucknow University, now called *Contemporary Social Work.*
1963	Indian Association of Trained Social Workers (IATSW) started publishing a journal called *Social Work Forum.*
1968	The first edition of *Encyclopaedia of Social Work in India* was published by the Planning Commission.
1981	*Social Work Forum* stopped being published.
1984	A journal called *Perspectives in Social Work* was started by the College of Social Work of the Nirmala Niketan Institute.
1987	The second edition of *Encyclopaedia of Social Work in India* was published by the Ministry of Welfare.
2000	*National Journal of Professional Social Work* was started by the Indian Society of Professional Social Work.

'Literature for social work' has to go beyond 'social work literature'. Social work profession has to base its work on the understanding of social phenomena as studied by various social sciences. Reality needs to be understood holistically in order to plan intervention. Multidisciplinary literature developed as applied social science on issues and problems is more directly useful for social work than literature focusing on one discipline's understanding of a phenomenon. Such literature is growing fast with the proliferation of non-government organisations and action groups. Literature of professions such as home science, psychiatry, law, and others are also useful for social work.

In spite of a need for practice-based literature for social work, research-based and social science books and journals are still considered the main media of knowledge for social work by publishers and libraries. As a result, the recent trend is to bring out the practice-based literature in unpublished forms. This practice makes dissemination and retrieval of this literature difficult. The libraries generally get books and journals and, that too, the foreign publications more easily than the Indian ones. Literature for social work is generally developed and disseminated by the Western countries, predominantly by the US and in English. Development of a profession requires a local and regional context and language orientation as well as international perspectives. However, Indian social work professionals, by and large, do not write; all that they write does not get published, and a lot of published literature does not get marketed. Social work knowledge development and its dissemination, thus remain weak in India, even in the age of information technology.

Summary Chart 6

Influences on Ideologies of Professional Social Work in India

Western Ideology of Professional Social Work	→	*Indian Ideologies for Social Change*	→	*Ideology of Professional Social Work in India*
Focus on individuals		Focus on families and communities		Focus on individuals, families and communities
Freedom as a goal		Duties as goals		Freedom and duties as goals
Importance of scientism		Importance of wisdom		Importance of scientism and wisdom
Theories, models and techniques for intervention		People's literature: stories, songs and art for social change		Theories, models and techniques and people's literature
Professional social workers take a salary		Voluntary social workers do not take a salary		Voluntary and professional, both types of social workers work

Module 5

Contemporary Ideologies for Social Change

TEACHER/LEARNER OBJECTIVES

The module on 'Contemporary Ideologies for Social Change' may have the following teacher/learner objectives:

1. Examine the transition from liberalism to the hegemonic ideology of neo-liberalism, leading to globalisation in the contemporary times.
2. Compare the emerging ideology of postmodernism with that of modernism.
3. Analyse the ideologies that try to counter neo-liberalism, namely, second wave feminism, resurgence of the civil society, multiculturalism and sustainable and people-centred development.
4. Understand the ideologies and roles played by action groups, new social movements and non-government organisations.

NEO-LIBERALISM

Historical Context of Origin and Development

Colonisation of the Southern countries by the Northern countries during the 18th, 19th and 20th centuries, led to collapse of civilisations, genocide, enslavement, capture of resources, and subservience of economies. After the colonies achieved independence, the dichotomy of the 'colonisers' and the 'colonised' changed to that of the 'First World' or 'developed countries' and the 'Third World' or 'underdeveloped countries'. The communist countries comprised the 'Second World'. Even when the erstwhile colonial territories acquired the status of independent countries, they generally adopted the political system of their master nations (Sharma, 1998). The development plans of the ex-colonies followed the coloniser's liberal paradigm of economic development, based on production and consumption of physical goods. Such a development became an instrument of the privileged class. The rural production system became a colonised base for the extraction of surplus for the urban-industrial economy (Saldanha, 1995). The new hierarchical dichotomy broadly assumed the form of "urban-organised" versus the "rural-unorganised", the urban elite assuming the aura and the role of the imperialists (Sharma, 1998).

The falling of the Berlin wall, in 1989, was symbolic of the process of disintegration of actually existing socialism. It became more difficult henceforth to envisage alternatives to capitalism. This has more relevance to the Third World because it coincided with accelerated globalisation of its economies (Dietrich, 2000b). Largely victims of debt trap, by the International Monetary Fund and the World Bank, the ex-colonies were pressured to privatise, liberalise and globalise, as an extension of the development project.

Ideals, Rationale and Goals for Social Change

Globalisation is the natural outcome of the neo-liberalist ideology, which promotes minimum government interference and considers market as the sole social regulator (George, Ramakrishnan and Cheriyan, 1997). Korten (1999) has listed the following components of the vision of globalisation:

- The world's money, technology and markets are controlled and managed by gigantic global corporations.
- A common consumer culture unifies all people in a shared quest for material gratification.
- Corporations are free to act solely on the basis of profitability, without regard to national or local consequences.
- Relationships, both, individual and corporate, are defined entirely by the market.
- There are no loyalties to place and community.

The global economy arranges its global operations to produce products where costs are lowest, sell them where markets are more lucrative, and shift the resulting profits to where tax rates are least burdensome. This weakens the bargaining power of any given locality and shifts the balance of power from the local human interest to the global corporate interest. It weakens the community to free the market, eliminates livelihoods to create wealth, and destroys life to increase unneeded and often unsatisfying consumption (Korten, 1999).

Critique and Implications

Neo-liberalism is modern colonialism, which won its great victories, not so much through its military and technological prowess, as through its ability to create secular hierarchies. These believe in the absolute superiority of the human over the non-human, the masculine over the feminine, the adult over the child, the historical over the ahistorical, and the modern progressive over the traditional or the savage (Nandy, 1998).

The appeal of neo-liberalism is usually based on the idea that implies less red tape, less centralisation and less bureaucratic control. However, the shift is from the rule of the nation-state to that of the global corporations. It implies less power to the people, because global corporations are more powerful than governments and also because they are less accountable than governments to democratic control (Shiva, 1997b). The most distinguishing feature of the global political economy at the moment is that people everywhere are pitched against a centralised system, which has assumed an identity independent of the people (Sharma, 1998).

A Manifesto of People's Global Action was prepared at a meeting of people's movements from all continents, in Geneva in 1998. According to this manifesto, the transnational corporations (TNCs) are taking over national enterprises, which most typically results in the destruction of jobs and dispossession of the workers of their ability to bargain with the capitalists in a national context. The TNCs are also violently invading the last refuges of indigenous peoples, violating their territories, habitats and resources, destroying their ways of life, and often perpetrating their genocide. The manifesto further observes that for decades, the institutions of the World Bank and the International Monetary Fund, and now the World Trade Organization (WTO), in alliance with national governments and corporate powers, have facilitated manoeuvrings to appropriate the environment.

Appropriation of environment has taken place as humans are considered above and outside of nature, as the source of all values, and nature is ascribed only an instrumental value (Capra, 1996). Shiva (1997b) noted that the end of the 'license *raj*' heralds the beginning of a 'patent *raj*'. Bio-diversity, land and water are the three vital resources that the majority of our people depend on for their livelihood and survival. "Intellectual property rights" are emerging as an important mechanism for taking away the living resources and bio-diversity from the people and converting them into corporate monopolies.

The result is environmental devastation, tragic and unmanageable social displacement and the wiping out of cultural and biological diversity, much of it irretrievably lost, without compensation to those reliant on it. Mass media and corporate consumerist culture are the main agents of commodification and homogenisation of cultural diversity. The domination of Western science and technology has swept away very diverse and valuable knowledge systems and technologies based on centuries of experience. Despite their many failures, capital-intensive technologies are systematically treated as superior to traditional labour-intensive technologies. This ideological discrimination results in unemployment and indebtedness. While the number of billionaires grows, more and more people around the world find themselves in a system that offers them no place in production and no access to consumption, even to meet their basic needs (People's Global Action, 1998).

Globalisation furthers the uninterrupted flow of resources from the Third World and, thus, aggravates the present unjust international economic order. It marginalises more and more sections of people as well as threatens bio-diversity and food security (George and others, 1997). The global business corporations propagate systems of values, thought, and law that favour the rights of property and capital over the rights of humans (Morehouse and Grossman, 1999). Each one of the multinationals can easily join the power game in smaller nation-states. They started playing the nefarious game of destabilising the systems which had hardly settled, removing any obstruction through conspiracy and even calculated political intervention. In most of the Third World countries, democratic institutions have been superseded by dictatorships which are at the mercy and under the command of global capitalist forces (Sharma, 1998). There is also evidence that violence and terrorism are associated with the redistribution of power from the political to the economic sector (Walz and Ritchie, 2000).

Several ideologies have emerged to counter neo-liberalism, as discussed below.

POSTMODERNISM

Postmodernists describe modern ideals of science, justice, and art, as ideals carrying with them specific political agenda and ultimately unable to legitimise themselves as universals. The claim is that the pursuit of such theories itself rests upon the modernist conception of a transcendent reason, a reason able to separate itself from the body and from historical time and place. Thus postmodernists recognise the highest ideals of modernity in the West as immanent to a specific historical time and geographical region and also associated with certain political baggage. Such a baggage includes notions of the supremacy of the West, of the legitimacy of science to tell us how to use our bodies, and of the distinction between art and mass culture (Nicholson, 1990).

Postmodernism challenges the modern, global, all-encompassing world views, be they political, religious or social, as meta-narratives that anticipate all questions and provide predetermined answers. Postmodernists, thus, reject attempts to apply the model of natural science inquiry in the social sciences (Rosenau, 1992). They critique totality, reason and universality and claim that in the name of "science", authority has been exercised in a variety of ways: in the disciplines, the media, popular advice manuals, and so on (Nicholson, 1990). Postmodernism is a discourse of plurality, difference and multinarratives. The postmodern reaction to modern ethical theories recommends that moral thinkers should turn their attention away from the problematic to the people as a whole. People's goodness has to do, not with virtues, but with their integrated wholeness (Agarwal, 1998). Postmodernists replace efforts at impartial observation with confidence in emotion, and prefer relativism to objectivity (Rosenau, 1992).

Postmodernism provides forms of historical knowledge as a way of reclaiming power and identity for subordinate groups (Giroux, 1991). The ideology of postmodernism has brought about visibility to important ideological and structural forces, such as race, gender and class, by acknowledging the question of power and value in the construction of knowledge and subjectivities. It has raised questions regarding how culture is inscribed in the production of centre/margin hierarchies and the reproduction of post-colonial forms of subjugation. The postmodernist thinking has led to a multidimensional understanding of social stratification, based on race, gender, education, and occupation, and not merely on class (Grusky and Takata, 1992).

Earlier, property relations obscured ethnic ones, but now it is property that begins to seem derivative and ethnicity that seems to become a more fundamental source of stratification (Grusky and Takata, 1992). Society has generally hierarchically ordered the ethnic groups, with typically a dominant or superordinate group and a subordinate group. Cultural explanations of ethnic inequalities impute "desirable" characteristics to the dominant groups such as ethnic purity and "undesirable" characteristics to the subordinate group to rationalise the hierarchy (Alba, 1992). Racism and the Indian caste system are clear examples of social stratification based on ethnicity and culture that has led to economic inequality. The tribals are imputed a low status also because of their cultural "backwardness" with reference to "development".

FEMINISM

Historical Context of Origin and Development

During the 19th century, the liberalist ideology led to the emergence of liberal feminism, the first school of feminist thought. The second wave feminism is dated from 1969 onwards. The United Nations Declaration of 1974 as the International Women's Year and 1976-85 as the International Decade for Women have led to a worldwide feminist movement (Marshall, 1994).

Perception of People and Social Problems

Feminists differentiate between sex as a biological division between men and women and gender as the socially unequal division into femininity and masculinity (Marshall, 1994). Gender has for long been treated as purely a "secondary force" in history. The presumption was that modern society is essentially a class system. The nuclear family was seen as the elemental unit of stratification, with the occupation or employment status of the family 'head' (that is the husband) defining the class position of all its members (Grusky and Takata, 1992). Feminism argues that the gender system subordinates women in patriarchal relations that exist over and above class relations, since male dominance over women's productive and reproductive roles predates the emergence of capitalism (O'Rand, 1992).

There are different schools of feminist thinking that have historically emerged. Liberal feminism is the oldest school, which emphasised the similarities of women with men and, therefore, demanded legal reforms and equal opportunities for suffrage, education, and employment. It achieved significant changes in these areas over a period of time. This school of thought dominates state policies in different countries even today. However, liberal feminists do not analyse the roots of gender oppression in society.

Marxist feminists view women's oppression as the outgrowth of the capitalist mode of production, which resulted in the spatial divide between domestic work and wage work and labelled them as non-productive and productive, respectively. Radical feminists identified the concern for patriarchal control over women's sexuality and reproduction. Issues of work and labour are seen by them as secondary. It is they who conceptualised patriarchy as a system of gender oppression. Socialist feminists attempt to synthesise Marxist thought with that of radical feminism, using the comprehensive tool of patriarchy as the system that controls women's labour, sexuality and reproduction (Poonacha, 1995).

Born out of women's experience of powerlessness, feminist ideologies today seek to understand the nature of power as it operates in women's lives. They attempt to explain not just the origins of gender subordination, but also the tenacity of such normative values in a changing socioeconomic scenario. These explanations go beyond sexism, to provide different perspectives on all kinds of social exclusion, including racism and casteism. The underlying contention is that the perceived disparities between the sexes is the earliest known form of social differentiation, it provides the script for the development of other known forms of oppressive practices (Poonacha, 1995).

Eco-feminists see the patriarchal domination and exploitation of women as the prototype of all domination and exploitation, including exploitation of nature. Accordingly, eco-feminists see female experiential knowledge as a major source for an ecological vision of reality (Capra, 1996).

Ideals, Rationale and Goals for Social Change

According to Bhasin and Khan (1986), anyone who recognises the existence of sexism, male domination or patriarchy, in society, and who takes some action to change the situation, is a feminist. They emphasised that feminists not only ask and fight for equality, dignity and freedom of choice to control their lives and bodies, but for a just society for women and men, both.

Brandwein (1990) listed the following interrelated components of feminism: Feminists see the world in a holistic way, encompassing macro- and micro-levels. Emerging from a holistic approach is a process-orientation, rejecting the ends/means split, emphasising the connection between the individual and her/his community. This leads to the importance of unity in diversity. By rejecting an either-or approach, feminists prefer a win-win rather than a win-lose approach to conflict, as power is seen as an empowerment of self, rather than control over others. A consensual, inclusionary decision making process and authority structure is, therefore, compatible with feminism. Finally, feminism implies a respect for nature, which does not exist just for human beings. Thus, feminism means replacing an outmoded value system with an alternative way of viewing the world. Feminism challenges all kinds of dichotomies that create hierarchies -- between public and private, mind and body, emotional and rational, qualitative and quantitative, and which ascribe lower value to all those attributes that are considered feminine (Bhaiya and Menon-Sen, 1996).

RESURGENCE OF THE CIVIL SOCIETY

The relative autonomy of civil society, that is various communities and collectives of people, often informal and inarticulate, is being perceptibly eroded by the advancing process of overbearing economic, political and cultural influences of remote forces (Roy, 1997). According to Srinivasan (1994), the growing pre-eminence of the state as an agency of centralised social and political control, led to homogenisation and unification of society and the state. He noted that an alien system of rational, centralised state government was imposed on the complex and heterogeneous realities of Indian society. All other forms of solidarity – linguistic, regional, communal – were defined in advance as representing a rudimentary polity, which is doomed historically. As the indigenous tradition is neither a fossil nor an empty sentiment but a conscious structure of knowledge and experience, nation-building is a coercive logic of indigenous institutional and ideological replacement. It is responsible for the cultural diversities to raise their heads as 'problems' of casteism, communalism and regionalism (Srinivasan, 1994).

According to Vandana Shiva (1997a), the centralised nation-state is anti-democratic and the representative democracy is inadequate to protect people's interests in a period of globalisation. The ideology of democratic pluralism recognises that diverse communities have diverse interests, they all have legitimate democratic rights of decision making and self-determination in matters that affect their lives, she stated. In fact, as Capra (1996) noted, the ethnic and cultural diversities contribute to the viability of the human society.

The Manifesto of People's Global Action (1998) states the following aims of joint actions against WTO, "free trade" and corporate rule:

- Taking back control of the means of production from the hands of both transnational and national capital, in order to create free, sustainable and community-controlled livelihoods, based on solidarity and people's needs and not on exploitation and greed.
- Accepting only those technologies, which can be managed, operated and controlled by local peoples.
- Rejecting the principle of competitiveness as a solution of people's problems.
- Respecting the right of indigenous peoples to territorial autonomy.
- A decentralised economy and polity based on communities' rights to natural resources and to plan their own

development, with equality and self-reliance as the basic values.

- Respecting traditional knowledge and cultures consonant with the values of equality, justice, and sustainability, evolving creative ways to use and fairly distribute natural resources.
- Taking control over culture, out of corporate hands, and reclaiming it by communities.
- Celebrating diversity of cultures and communities and place none above the other.

MULTICULTURALISM

There is an inherent tendency in, both, the liberal democratic state and the global market economy to run down pluralism. Ends of both are served through homogenisation of citizen responses and social tastes. In India, the homogenisation is being defined and determined in terms of fictional majoritarian conceptions and values of Hinduism (Ahmad, 1998).

According to Bhargava (1999), multiculturalism is a move away from the modern ideology, which concerned itself with freedom, equality and justice, given a pronounced individualist colouring. The framework of material welfare and a culturally-neutral universalism underscores the importance of individual choice, the compulsion of a more equitable distribution of material resources and the need to belong to a wider social and political universe, where neither one's class or status nor cultural inheritance was a source of advantage or disadvantage. Here, the dominant cultures generate stereotypes of the dominated which they get their victims to accept and that results in the loss of confidence and pervasive self-images of inferiority. People then lose respect for their own cultures and hasten the progress of homogenisation, induced by dominant cultures (Bhargava, 1999).

The belated recognition has come that culture-relative self-esteem matters to people as much as the fulfilment of material needs. Multiculturalism brings together issues that relate to the need for community, a sense of belonging to it, the importance of a secure sense of identity, of status and recognition, of particularity and the need to recognise and maintain difference with others. This is the framework of identity and cultural particularity. Both sameness and difference can be a source of inequality and injustice. We must neither be discriminated on account of particular features of religion and culture, nor, as a condition of citizenship, be compelled to set aside our cultural particularity (Bhargava, 1999).

Thus, the communitarian standpoint questioned a political order constructed purely from the vantage point of individual well-being. The importance of cultural particularity raised doubts about the desirability of a unicultural polity. Multiculturalism opposes cultural imperialism and homogenisation and opposes states whose only objectives are the survival and well-being of the dominant cultural group. A demand to renounce cultural identity as a condition for free and equal citizenship no longer appears to be viable. Recent demands for a multicultural society constitute a plea for egalitarian multiculturalism. Egalitarian multiculturalism requires recognition or respect for culture, which in turn is possible only after a degree of interaction, familiarity and mutual understanding. Communal politics thrive on false stereotypes, which constrain rather than help intercultural understanding (Bhargava, 1999).

Democracy needs a common identity: for people to be sovereign, a new self-understanding among individuals, as collective agents, who are more than a mere disparate set of individuals, must come into existence. Unless this happens, little reason exists for people to accept the decisions of the majority. The unity required for collective agency is antecedently achieved by culture or ethnicity. The very requirements of collective agency central to the democratic vision, simultaneously generate the temptation to nurture a strongly exclusionary ethnic or cultural nationalism. The democratic age itself poses new obstacles to coexistence, which was possible to achieve within an undemocratic political structure (Bhargava, 1999).

IDEOLOGIES OF SUSTAINABLE AND PEOPLE-CENTRED DEVELOPMENT

Capra (1996) promoted the ideology that the world is not a collection of isolated objects, but a network of phenomena that are fundamentally interconnected and interdependent. In nature there is no "above" or "below", and there are no hierarchies. There are only networks nesting within other networks. Ultimately, such deep ecological awareness is spiritual or religious awareness, he said. According to him, the principles of the planet's ecosystems organise themselves to maximise sustainability through interdependence, recycling, partnership, flexibility, and diversity. The same principles can be used as guidelines to build sustainable human communities.

Sustainable development is a process in which economic, fiscal, trade, energy, agricultural, industrial and all other policies are designed to bring about development that is economically, socially, and ecologically sustainable. This means that current consumption cannot be financed for long by incurring economic debts that others must repay. It also means that enough must be invested in the education and health of today's generation to avoid creating a social debt for future generations. Moreover, it means that natural resources must be used in ways that do not create ecological debts by overexploiting the earth's carrying and productive capacity. All postponed debts – whether economic, social or ecological – mortgage sustainability (Haq, 1998).

People-centred development is a vision that is an expression of people's awareness, aspiration and struggles and, therefore, sustainable. This vision accepts that people are knowledgeable about their situation and how to manage them, given the necessary resources. It acknowledges that people have the right to plan their own destinies and determine their own lifestyles. It appreciates that local solutions must be congruent with local resource realities at the time, both geographical and human (Cox, 1993).

IDEOLOGIES OF ACTION GROUPS AND NEW SOCIAL MOVEMENTS

Ideologies of Action Groups

Historical Context of Origin

Post-1960s, stagnation of the economy with the marginalisation of vast numbers in the unorganised and rural sectors of the society became apparent. The state and the political institutions, though highly centralised, were seen to have lost their capacity to direct market forces (Saldanha, 1995). Since the 1970s, large number of people started action groups, influenced by Paulo Freire, whose thought and work spread from the North East of Brazil to the entire world, and made a profound impact in the overall struggle for liberation (Schaull, 1972).

Benefactors and their Motives

Sen (1998) classified the people who formed action groups during the 1960s and the 1970s into six types:

- Educated middle class youth, who were dissatisfied with the model of development adopted by the state and politics of leftist parties.

- Officials of the existing non-profit organisations that were involved in the modern projects in the 1960s, who were disillusioned with developmental projects, which did little to alleviate poverty.
- Younger followers of the Sarvoday movement which lost momentum in the late 1970s.
- Ex-Naxalites who were disillusioned with the fragmentation of the Naxalite movement by Indira Gandhi's government with the help of the army and police by the mid-1970s.
- Indian Christians influenced by liberation theology.
- New Left academics influenced by Western Marxist thought, who mainly formed documentation and research centres and provided advice and training to the action groups.

Ideology of Paulo Freire

Paulo Freire's early sharing of the life of the poor led him to the discovery of what he describes as the 'culture of silence' of the dispossessed. He came to realise that their ignorance and lethargy were the direct products of the whole situation of economic, social and political domination – and of the paternalism -- of which they were victims. Rather than being encouraged and equipped to know and respond to the concrete realities of their world, they were kept 'submerged' in a situation in which such critical awareness and response were practically impossible. It became clear to him that the whole educational system was one of the major instruments for the maintenance of this culture of silence (Schaull, 1972).

Freire wrote in 1972 that dehumanisation is the result of an unjust order that engenders violence in the oppressors, which, in turn, dehumanises the oppressed. Because it is a distortion of being fully human, sooner or later, being less human leads to the oppressed to struggle against those who made them so. In order for this struggle to have meaning, the oppressed must not, in seeking to regain their humanity, become in turn oppressors of the oppressors, but rather restorers of the humanity of both. This, then, is the great humanistic and historical task of the oppressed: to liberate themselves and their oppressors as well. The oppressors, who oppress, exploit and rape by virtue of their power, cannot find in this power the strength to liberate either the oppressed or themselves. Any attempt to 'soften' the power of the oppressor in deference to the weakness of the oppressed almost always manifests itself in the form of false generosity. True generosity consists precisely in fighting to destroy the causes, which nourish false charity.

According to Freire (1972), the oppressed, having internalised the image of the oppressors and adopted their guidelines, are fearful of freedom. The 'fear of freedom' may lead them to desire the role of the oppressor or bind them to the role of the oppressed. Freedom would require them to eject this image and replace it with autonomy and responsibilities. Self-deprecation is another characteristic of the oppressed, which derives from their internalisation of the opinion the oppressors hold of them. Those who work for liberation, must not take advantage of the emotional dependence of the oppressed. Libertarian action must recognise this dependence as a weak point and must attempt through reflection and action to transform it into independence. The conviction of the oppressed that they must fight for their liberation is not a gift bestowed by the revolutionary leadership, but the result of their own conscientisation. To surmount the situation of oppression, human beings must first critically recognise its causes, so that, through transforming action, they can create a new situation – one which makes pursuit of a fuller humanity possible.

Freire (1972) observed that certain members of the oppressor class join the oppressed in their struggle for liberation. When they do so, they always bring with them the marks of their origin: their prejudices and their deformations, which include a lack of confidence in the people's ability to think, to want, and to know. They believe that they must be the executors of the transformation. Only through comradeship with the oppressed, can the converts understand their characteristic ways of living and behaving, which in diverse moments, reflect the structure of domination (Freire, 1972).

Freire (1972) developed a pedagogy of the oppressed, which must be forged with, not for, the oppressed in the incessant struggle to regain humanity. This pedagogy has two stages: In the first stage, the oppressed unveil the world of oppression and through the praxis commit themselves to its transformation. In the second stage, in which the reality of oppression has already been transformed, this pedagogy ceases to belong to the oppressed and becomes a pedagogy of all human beings in the process of permanent liberation.

Ideologies of New Social Movements

The number of action groups, their widespread character and the interlinkages that have developed among them have given rise to the new social movements (NSMs). Conceptually social movements and action groups are separable, though empirically there usually exists some relationship between the two. Action groups can be initiators of social movements but not necessarily their customary agents, instruments or carriers (Dhanagare, 1988).

Omvedt (1998) observes that the old movements, both the working class movement and the national anti-colonial movements, took as their model of development the industrial society of the West. The development project of the socialist revolutions was to create an industrial society and make it liberatory, democratic and socialist, through collective state ownership of the means of production. Besides globalisation and decline of the state, disintegration of the United Soviet Socialist Republic of Russia, weakened the socialist ideology in the world. This led to an immense subjective political and cultural withdrawal from class politics and class analysis (Omvedt, 1998). According to Dietrich (2000a), the new social movements are supposed to be governed by an overriding ideology that presents a systematised critique of modern society and of development, not only from strictly economic but also ecological perspectives (Dietrich, 2000a).

The NSMs are defined by Jose (1998) as movements that are against forms of exploitation, not recognised by the traditional class analysis. They question the claim of the proletariat to speak and act in the name of all disaffected groups and be in the vanguard of revolutionary social change. A critique/revaluation or an engagement with the socialist perspective is seen as necessary to characterise a social movement as 'new'. These seem to encourage a focus on 'community' rather than 'class', even when the demands are primarily economic. Race, gender and environment provide the context of identity politics of the NSMs.

The characteristics of NSMs are autonomy from the state and democratic internal functioning. The anti-statism of the NSMs, with its inherent distrust of electoral politics and political parties does not mean an anti-political essence but rather an effort to redefine political action, to reconstruct politics (Jose, 1998). Omvedt (1998) notes that the NSMs are primarily democratic revolutions, stressing various aspects of subordination and exploitation. In these revolutions, the democratic imaginary with the themes of liberty, equality, autonomy and so on, constitute the 'people' as the basis of political legitimacy as the major revolutionary force. Samir

Amin (1996) defined the direction for the NSMs as democratic re-politicisation of the masses, based on reinforcement of their capacity for self-organisation, self-development and self-defence. The attempt is to reduce the gap between "us" as the benefactors and "them" as the beneficiaries.

The NSMs began to identify at least in part with a critique of Hinduism and to put forward new cultural themes that began to converge with those of the Dalit movement. The growing challenges of religious fundamentalism everywhere made it necessary for democratic and revolutionary forces to deal with issues of identity. A consensus was developing that secularism could not remain an abstract ideal, but had to be identified with the popular traditions of communities (Omvedt, 1996). The NSM ideology is integrated with the quest for cultural pluralism and a political concept of participatory democracy versus politics of representation (Dietrich, 2000a).

The labour movement in India is basically the trade union movement, which is not able to respond to the new scenario where a large percentage of working class population is in the unorganised sector, coupled with steady decline in the organised work force (Bhowmick, 1998). Monteiro and Lingam (1998) note that while the labour movement has tended towards an economistic orientation, the Dalit, the tribal, the women's and the environmental movements have regarded the symbolic. The important realm of these struggles is in terms of reinterpretation of history, assertion of submerged linguistic and cultural identities, and affirmation of alternative symbols or cosmologies.

Types of NSMs

According to Teltumbde (2000), reservations in education, employment and politics, instead of strengthening Dalits, has emasculated them politically and caused the creation of a separate class of beneficiaries from amongst them, which if at all, has a very tenuous linkage with the Dalit masses. However, several Dalit organisations have come up, over a period of time, campaigning for Dalit rights. In 1972, the neo-Buddhists set up an organisation called the Dalit Panthers in Bombay, with the intention of working for the rights of the oppressed masses who were discriminated against and for a radical improvement of their standard of living. In 1992, the Dalit Solidarity Programme was initiated which aims at solidarity among Dalits belonging to different religions, regions, and sub-castes; works in close association with the tribals; brings necessary changes in the curriculum in the present education system; and internationalises the problem of Dalits (Ramaiah, 1998). The National Campaign on Dalit Human Rights actively and aggressively reaffirms that the untouchables are part of the original inhabitants in India and struggles for their rights within the framework of the Indian Constitution (Alex, 2001).

The women's movement has raised fundamental issues of structural and cultural oppression, which the class perspective had ignored earlier. The tribal movements aim at reaffirmation of identity, the struggle to recapture control over resources, a redefinition of the political domain and a redefinition of development. The emerging perspectives within the tribal movement signal a shift from resistance to resurgence, towards ethno-development (Prabhu, 1998). The environmental movement has established the linkage between the interests of the toiling people and natural resources over which their rights are shrinking continuously. A secular cultural movement is emerging around the agenda of anti-communalism (Bharucha, 1988).

The human rights discourse in India is characterised by a distinction between 'civil liberties' (rights of citizens against the state) and 'democratic rights' (expectations of entitlements of just governance, insisting on fulfilment of positive obligations of the state towards peoples). Civil rights impose restrictions on state power, while demands of democratic rights summon the state to pursue affirmative action empowering people. While civil rights are rights of citizens or persons, democratic rights are asserted in the name of the people or the masses. The political/intellectual Left tends to be associated with movements of democratic rights while the liberals are seen as crusaders for civil liberties. In situation of overall political crises, both activist streams co-mingle, but in times of peace there exists a deep divide between the two types of discursive struggles (Baxi, 1998). In 1974, Jayaprakash Narayan formed the Citizens for Democracy and in 1976, he formed the People's Union for Civil Liberties and Democratic Rights (PUCLDR). In 1981, PUCLDR split into PUCL comprised of elitists and PUDR comprised of Leftists.

The range of human rights movements includes those for children's rights, housing rights, health rights and literacy rights, among others. Rather than locate rights in the individualist tradition of Western liberalism they are seen as affirmation of political conditions of human existence that involves struggle against class exploitation and social oppression. The human rights movement has squarely exposed the authoritarian acts of the state and powerful social forces, and helped in connecting the various movements for the protection of democratic rights (Mohanty, 1998). However, as Muzaffar (1994) noted, while most human rights groups are concerned about authoritarianism at the national level, they seldom react to the control and dominance of world politics by a clique from the North.

The National Alliance of People's Movements (NAPM) was initiated after India adopted the New Economic Policy of liberalisation in 1991. There was a felt need to forge a grassroots alliance to oppose the hegemonic and exploitative onslaught of globalisation. It is a broad non-party political process to intervene in current socio-political processes. It proposes to bring the basic issues of development, alternative and sustainable development, and secularism, on the national agenda. With a broad national framework aiming at infusing a more people-oriented approach towards planning and development, the NAPM is seeking to prevent the mistakes of the past by working for a more equitable attitude in policy-making (Menon, 1995).

The NAPM advocates cancellation of debts and quitting of the WTO, side by side with sustainable agriculture, decentralised industries, *gram swaraj* (village self governance), drastic social reform and organisation of unorganised sector of workers. It defends the right to know and basic democratic organisational processes that go beyond party politics and electioneering. Different ideological streams of socialists, Gandhians, Marxists, Phule-Ambedkarite Dalit ideologies and feminists have come together and been involved in a patient process of common struggles and ideological battles. This has created considerable ferment of debate, campaigning and united struggles. One of its most important contribution is the creation of a focus on alternative development (Dietrich, 2000a). However, the Manifesto of People's Global Action (1998) note that transnational capital can not be confronted with the traditional tools used in the national context. Only globalised alliance of peoples' movements can defeat the emerging global monster.

IDEOLOGIES OF NON-GOVERNMENT ORGANISATIONS

As the limitations of state-sponsored, project-based, top-down development became apparent, the 1980s and the 1990s saw increasing attention focussed on private, professional development organisations called non-government organisations (NGOs). NGO is a United Nations term coined mainly to indicate the difference between the organisations of the states, which are its direct members, and the organisations that do not belong to the state. Privatisation and globalisation catapulted the NGOs onto centre stage, often according them a major role in dealing with the new social, economic, political and environmental concerns (Voluntary Action Network India, nd). The founding members of the NGOs that came up in the 1980s and the 1990s were still the middle class or lower middle class professionals and quasi-professionals.

The Seventh Five Year Plan (1985-90) granted formal recognition to NGOs. The 1980s and the 1990s also saw growth in the size and the number of NGOs, and diversification of its roles into three types:

- NGOs that concentrate on development while acting as intermediaries between donor agencies (including the government and foreign) and the poor.
- NGOs that concentrate on empowerment, which take initiatives to form community-based organisations (CBOs), help the poor obtain their rights from the state, organise them around issues that adversely affect them, and lobby for them at various levels of the state, form networks around popular issues and campaigns around issues such as energy, environment, housing or women's rights.
- NGOs as development consultants which provide training to smaller NGOs and CBOs, consulting services to governments and foreign agencies and conduct documentation and research.

Many radical scholars believe that funds from imperialistic countries proliferate voluntary groups, primarily to influence the course of development of the respective societies in which they operate, to systematically counter and weaken the potential of the Left Movement in these countries. It has shifted the main course of people's movement from 'liberation' to 'development' (Dhanagare, 1988).

Samuel (1998) criticises the term NGOs as a blanket term that appropriates diverse ideological, cultural, ethical, and institutional initiatives under an all-encompassing stereotype. It exemplifies the homogenising tendency of globalisation. It homogenises the whole social change spectrum. It sucks up various shades of experience into a dominant discourse dictated by a handful of multilateral developmental institutions in a handful of rich countries. Secondly, government is the reference point for the term. In the Indian historical context, voluntary organisations or social change initiatives have always treated people, rather than government, as the major reference point (Samuel, 1998).

According to Sethi (1998), the NGOs with specialised skills attempt to reach out both to the grassroots and the policy makers. Most of these new efforts depend strongly on an external infusion of funding, often international. Everyone, from the donor government, the social commentator and the middle class para-professionals, now find it lucrative to enter the 'grassroots business', in the process, hegemonising the voice of the grassroots. The internal criteria of validations, that people whom you work with should support you, are replaced by donor-sensitive criteria. Rajni Kothari (1989) noted that there has taken place a striking growth of individualism and egotism among activists and professionals and the draw of material incentives.

Summary Chart 7

Understanding Neo-liberalism

Goals and Outcomes of Neo-liberalism

Goals	*Outcomes*
Focus on rights of property	Neglect of rights of humans
Freeing of the market	Weakening of the community
Creation of wealth	Elimination of livelihoods
Increase in consumption	Destruction of life
Reduction in rule of the state	Increase in rule of the global corporations
Homogenisation	Wiping out of cultural and biological diversity
Freedom from control of licenses	Control of intellectual property rights

Hierarchial Dichotomies created by Liberalism

Worthy	Non-worthy
Deserving	Not deserving
Haves	Have-nots
Civilised	Primitive
Advanced	Backward
Scientific	Superstitious
Colonisers	Colonised
Developed	Underdeveloped
Urban-organised	Rural-unorganised

Summary Chart 8

Modernism versus Postmodernism and their Implications

Modernism	Postmodernism
Rational	Intuitive
Focus on problematics	Focus on people as integrated wholes
Science for knowledge	Community-based consciousness
Impartial observation	Confidence in emotion
Objectivity	Relativism
Analysis	Synthesis
Linear	Non-linear
Reductionist	Holistic
Meta-narratives	Multinarratives
Universality	Plurality
Implications	
Expansion	Conservation
Competition	Cooperation
Domination	Partnership

Summary Chart 9

Key Foci and Implications of Contemporary Ideologies

Contemporary Ideologies	*Key Foci*	*Implications*
Neo-Liberalism	Minimum government interference and market as the sole social regulator, rule of global corporations, independent of the people	Creation of secular hierarchies Elimination of livelihood Wiping out of cultural and biological diversity
Postmodernism	Viewing people as integrated wholes, community-based consciousness, confidence in emotion, relativism, synthesis, non-linear, multinarratives and plurality	Promotion of conservation, cooperation and partnership Deconstruction of professional power
Feminism	Recognition of male domination and subordination of women's labour, sexuality and reproduction	Challenge to all dichotomies that create hierarchies
Resurgence of civil society	Resurgence of autonomy of communities and collectives of peoples	Promotion of local self-governance and direct democracy
Multiculturalism	Opposition of cultural imperialism and homogenisation	Promotion of egalitarian multiculturalism
Ideologies of sustainable and people-centred development	Development that aims at sustainability through interdependence, recycling, partnership, flexibility, and diversity with people at the centre of planning	Economic, social and ecological sustainability for future generations

Contd...

Contd...

Contemporary Ideologies	*Key Foci*	*Implications*
Ideologies of action groups	Conscientisation of the oppressed about their victimisation through economic, social and political domination	Libertarian action to transform the dependence of the oppressed into independence who will fight for their own liberation
Ideologies of labour movements	The trade union movement has had an economic orientation	Cannot respond to the needs of the large and increasing unorganised work force
Ideologies of new social movements	Focus on community rather than class identity politics with reference to race and gender, critique of development from the economic and ecological perspectives	Democratic repoliticisation of the masses, focus on alternative development
Ideologies of human rights movements	Expose the authoritarian acts of the state and powerful social forces	Help in connecting the various movements
Ideologies of non-government organisations	Intermediation between donors and the poor Empowerment of the poor Development consultants	Major role in welfare and development compared to the state, homogenisation of voluntary sector, donor-sensitivity and accountability more important than people-sensitivity and accountability

Module 6

Contemporary Ideologies of Social Work Profession

TEACHER/LEARNER OBJECTIVES

The module on 'Contemporary Ideologies of Social Work Profession' may have the following teacher/learner objectives:

1. Summarise the ideologies for social change that have lead to marginalisation of vulnerable groups and their problems and understand that the same ideologies have led to professionalisation of social work, so the profession has limitations in dealing with these problems.
2. Summarise the contemporary ideologies that are trying to counter the marginalising ideologies and examine their linkages to professional social work.
3. Analyse the contemporary process of systemic marginalisation of vulnerable groups through prejudicing ideologies, linked to access to resources and power, and reinforced by social systems.

4. Examine the emerging ideologies of social work profession and the challenges in realising their ideals.

IDEOLOGIES THAT HAVE MARGINALISED VULNERABLE GROUPS

According to the theory of historical materialism, the changes in the mode of production have brought about changes in the societal structure, institutionalising different forms of inequality. In the agriculture and horticulture phase, need for labour led to the practice of marriage, slavery, and feudalism, institutionalising inequality, justified by sexism and racism. When paternity was discovered through domestication of animals, and labour was needed for agriculture, by landed classes, patriliny through marriage was introduced. In the slavery system, those who were impoverished and became economically dependent on their kinsmen or fellow tribesfolk, through debts, were turned into slaves. Slavery gave way to feudalism, which became an important feature of the medieval period.

In the West, secular humanism and Protestantism revived the importance of human beings, as against religion and work ethics, but promoted individualism. Rationalism led to emergence of scientism and launched several modern ideologies. With the change in the predominant production process from agricultural to industrial, in the modern period, industries needed labour that was tied to the land. The political control of the landowning aristocracy and monarchies was challenged and foundations were laid for the modern nation-states (Ram, 1999). Individual merit was considered the determinant of status in the new class-stratification of the capitalist and the labour. However, this does not happen in practice, since the majority have already been deprived of the means of production and, therefore, also of the fruits of production (Kappen, 1994). The Industrial Revolution made European nationalism aggressive and expansionist, promoting international trade and colonisation of Asian and African countries. The pre-eminence of the nation-states grew as agencies of centralised social and political control, representing the interest of the capitalists against the people.

Utilitarianism and Social Darwinism promoted international trade, justified colonisation, leading to Industrial Revolution in the West, and established the capitalistic paradigm of development all over the world, dividing it into the First World and the Third World. Socialism tried to counter the uncontrolled growth of liberalistic ideologies, that led to the emergence of the Second World. Domination of the liberalistic lobby in the development and implementation of the United Nations human rights instruments after the Second World War, further promoted individualism and liberalism. Recently, the transition from liberalism to the hegemonic ideology of neo-liberalism has led to creation of secular hierarchies, elimination of livelihoods and wiping out of cultural and biological diversity, under the name of globalisation.

LIMITATIONS OF PROFESSIONAL SOCIAL WORK

The Western modern ideologies, that have led to marginalisation of vulnerable groups, have also led to requirements of a profession such as social work in terms of secularisation of help and importance of scientific knowledge, formal education and specialisations, the liberalistic context of predominance of the clinical approach in social work profession in the US and its implications for support from the capitalists and the state. Such a profession has limitations in dealing with the social problems created by the same ideologies.

In the 1970s, there was an increase in the number of people who felt that social work in particular was irrelevant, that it had no impact on the daily lives of the poor and handicapped and might even do damage by seeming to achieve something in a kind of public relations exercise. Influenced by the emerging philosophies for social change, radical social workers saw their profession as part of the problem rather than its solution (Brandon, 1976).

A National Conference was organised by TISS in 1996, on Movements and Campaigns for the Empowerment of the Marginalised Groups to celebrate its 60 years. The following observations were made at this conference, by the activists, whether professionally trained in social work or not (TISS, 1997):

- Social work practice has got reduced to methods of casework, group work and community organisation and service delivery systems.
- Practice, social science research and education in social work are fragmented.
- Professionalisation has led to elitism and ideology has taken a back seat in social work.
- Social work is depoliticised so social action is neglected.
- Interface of social work with social movements/campaigns is weak.

CONTEMPORARY IDEOLOGIES FOR SOCIAL CHANGE AND PROFESSIONAL SOCIAL WORK

In order to counter the limitations of professional social work, radical and progressive paradigms have emerged in social work, as discussed below. The profession is in the process of learning from the thinking of Karl Marx, Paulo Freire and Gandhiji and the contemporary ideologies that are trying to counter the marginalising ideologies, namely, postmodernism, second wave feminism, resurgence of the civil society, multiculturalism and sustainable and people-centred development and the roles being played by action groups, new social movements and non-government organisations.

Radical Social Work

Radical social work emerged in the 1970s, due to the influence of Marxist theory, particularly in Europe and Latin America. It proposed that social distress arises from the oppression of the working class by the capitalist elites (Payne, 2000). Its ideology is that the most effective way to achieve goals of equality and solutions to social problems is to eliminate or make major changes in the existing institutions. It includes techniques for peaceably bringing about these changes, including passive resistance, demonstrations, strikes and political and social activism (Barker, 1987).

Progressive Social Work

Progressive social workers may identify themselves as radicals, socialists, leftists, political practitioners, or activists. They are critical of the injustices in institutions, systems, beliefs, and social practices that cause the poorest and most-vulnerable groups to suffer. They articulate these social injustices into "public issues" instead of adopting a strictly case-by-case perspective that views the outcomes of social injustices as "personal troubles", that individuals must cope with or adapt to (Mills, 1959, cited from Bombyk, 1995). Progressive social workers strive to alter oppressive institutions, systems, beliefs, and practices fundamentally by initiating social changes targeted at these public issues. They also work directly with individuals to help them heal from their wounds, to educate them about their life choices and strategies, and to assist them as they determine their futures (Bombyk, 1995).

Feminist Social Work

Feminist social work is the integration of the values, skills and knowledge of social work with a feminist orientation to help individuals and society overcome the emotional and social problems that result from sex discrimination (Barker, 1987). By placing gender on the social work map, feminist social workers have challenged the gender neutrality regarding the social divisions usually upheld in traditional social work theories and practice (Dominelli, 2002). It also helps social work professionals to undertake a holistic approach and challenge all dichotomies that create hierarchies.

Postmodernism and Social Work

In modernism, social work found a belief that if we could be 'scientific' enough, we could locate the causes of our clients' miseries, with a high level of certainty and intervene appropriately to eliminate the problems. However, it has not brought us a better world. Postmodernism has brought an epistemological revolution, a new level of freedom and intellectual creativity to social work thought, practice, research and teaching (Laird, 1994).

Postmodern concepts enable social work practitioners to situate themselves as potential oppressors. These are useful for them to examine the complexities of power in 'client'-worker relationship, reinforcement of mainstream middle class norms in assessment processes and so on. These help social workers to create empowering relationships by deconstructing professional power, which stems from their position as bearers of particular ideologies and implementers of a social mandate, determined in the political arena (Dominelli, 2002). Besides deconstruction of professional power, postmodernism also promotes values of viewing people as integrated wholes, community-based consciousness, confidence in emotion, relativism, synthesis, multinarratives, plurality, conservation, cooperation and partnership, that are useful for social work profession.

According to Roche and others (1999), social work today straddles the modernist and postmodernist treatments of knowledge. In the first, it proffers professional knowledge of technical concepts, theories, and methods, and in the second, it is a reflective, generative process of constructive meaning from multiple viewpoints.

Other Contemporary Ideologies and Social Work

The values of local self-governance and direct democracy; egalitarian multiculturalism; economic, social and ecological sustainability, through interdependence, recycling, partnership, flexibility and diversity, with people at the centre of planning; conscientisation of the oppressed about their victimisation, through economic, social and political domination, and libertarian action to transform the dependence of the oppressed into independence who will fight for their own liberation; focus on alternative development; protest against the authoritarian acts of the state and powerful social forces and so on, need to be adopted by social work professionals also. Social work professionals also need to be cautious of the temptations of the donor-driven non-government organisations and discourage their homogenisation.

CONTEMPORARY PROCESS OF SYSTEMIC MARGINALISATION OF VULNERABLE GROUPS

Social workers need to understand and be sensitive to how in contemporary times also prejudicing ideologies, their own and in others, marginalise the vulnerable groups, systemically. Prejudicing ideologies assume physical and mental capabilities, which justify role stereotypes, based on certain constructs. The role stereotypes influence people's access to resources, that result in differential power. Power determines status in a hierarchical form, which leads to discrimination, intolerance and even justifies violence against the powerless at the lowest rungs of the hierarchies. Lower status, in turn, leads to differential access to resources, reaffirming role stereotypes and prejudices.

Prejudicing Ideologies

A prejudice most commonly refers to a negative or unfavourable attitude towards a group or its individual members. Over-generalisation, prejudgement, refusal to take account of individual differences and so on, place the individual or group at some disadvantage (Marshall, 1994). Prejudicing ideologies based on perception of inherent physical and mental incapability, based on age, ethnicity, sex, and class of individuals and/or groups, are respectively called ageism, ethnocentrism, sexism, classism, and so on. These 'isms' justify role stereotypes, hierarchy, intolerance, and discrimination and, thereby, justify violence. Prejudices restrict perception of dignity and worth, contribution of each individual in the universe, and make rights and opportunities conditional. Thus these prejudicing ideologies have led to vulnerability of women, children, elderly, disabled, Dalits and tribes, the non-white races and the poor classes. These are elaborated below.

Sexism

Sexism is a prejudice or discrimination on the grounds of sex, especially against women (*Reader's Digest Oxford*, 1993). It implies stereotypes of women's physical and mental capabilities which justify male control over women with reference to their labour, sexuality and reproductive roles. Sexism justifies role stereotypes of earner for the man and housewife for the woman, headship for the man and subordination for women, and discrimination and violence against women.

Ageism

Ageism is the holding of prejudicial views about individuals or groups based on their age (Marshall, 1994). Ageism implies assumptions about physical and mental incapability, mainly of children and elderly, which lead to role stereotypes of dependency, hierarchy, intolerance, discrimination and violence against them.

Ableism

Ableism is discrimination in favour of the able bodied (*Reader's Digest Oxford*, 1993). Ableism implies assumptions about physical and mental incapability of the visually, orthopaedically, audibly and the mentally differently-abled people, which lead to role stereotypes, hierarchy, intolerance, discrimination and violence against these people.

Ethnocentrism

Ethnocentrism is making judgements about other ethnic groups in terms of one's own cultural assumptions. It often suggests that the way something is done in other ethnic groups is inferior to the way it is done in one's own ethnic group (Marshall, 1994). It blocks recognition of other cultures as good and necessary for others as their own for themselves. Ethnocentrism is applicable to cultural and behavioural practices based on one's own religion, tribe, mother-tongue and regional origin. Ethnocentrism leads to ethnic stereotypes, intolerance, discrimination and violence against those with cultural background different than one's own.

Casteism, Racism and Eurocentrism

Casteism and racism are hierarchical concepts, where prejudice is about superiority or inferiority of other castes and races with reference to one's own. Brahminism views Brahmins and their practices as superior to those of the other castes. Eurocentrism is a tendency to view the European cultural practices as superior to all others. These prejudices also justify intolerance, discrimination and violence against those at the lower rungs of the hierarchy, especially Dalits and blacks. Eurocentrism has led to marginalisation of all the non-European people.

Classism

Classism is based in the liberal ideology and implies prejudices with reference to socio-economic class, with specific reference to its association with qualifications, respectability of occupation and morals, and blaming the poor for their poverty and for other social problems. Classism also justifies role stereotypes, hierarchy, intolerance, discrimination and violence against the poverty groups.

Resources and Power

Prejudicing ideologies determine people's access to resources, justified by role stereotypes. Social status is a derivation of power of control over resources. The following are varied types of resources that lead to power (adapted from Batliwala, 1993):

Resources	*Power*
Physical	might, military, institutionalisation
Natural	land, water, forests
Economic	income, assets, capital
Political	membership of parliament/cabinet/bureaucracy
Intellectual	information, education, technology
Cultural	beliefs, values, ideology
Self	self-image, confidence

Groups or systems that have control over resources also have control over the prejudicing ideology that influence role and resource allocation. The vulnerable groups are powerless with reference to control over resources due to the roles that they have historically performed, which are justified by the prejudicing ideologies of the dominant groups. Weber regarded power as the fundamental concept in stratification. Status is a kind of normatively defined social power. He defined power as the probability of persons or groups carrying out their will even when opposed by others (Marshall, 1994).

Systems of Marginalisation

Family, religion, society, state, and the national and global systems of market systematise and perpetuate stratification and marginalisation. With an open and permeable boundary, social systems are in constant interaction with their environment. With inputs from the environment, systems tend to change but strive for homeostasis for self-preservation, by making adaptations. Their output to the environment is fed back by the environment as input into the systems, forming feedback loops. These loops create non-linear interconnectedness attempting towards achieving equilibrium among systems (Capra, 1982). Prejudicing ideologies leading to role, power and status allocation to individuals or sub-systems, thus get reinforced and further differentiated by the role, power and status allocation, leading to systemic marginalisation.

EMERGING IDEOLOGIES OF PROFESSIONAL SOCIAL WORK AND THE CHALLENGES AHEAD

Declaration of Ethics for Professional Social Workers

With the emergence of action groups and new social movements, an activist orientation has emerged in social work in India. Some professional social workers have joined social action groups, whereas some have started their own action groups. Some have been making a contribution through teaching and research in academic institutions, and some have been working through international organisations. With the growing trend towards activist social work in India, the social work professionals questioned the clinically-oriented code of ethics (by NASW) that they had been using in social work education for a long time.

The 'Declaration of Ethics for Professional Social Workers', of 1997, was prepared by the Social Work Educators Forum at TISS (TISSSWEF, 1997), with inputs from its faculty members, participants of a national workshop on social work practice and education, members of the faculty of the College of Social Work at Nirmala Niketan, members of the Bombay Association of Trained Social Workers and some retired social work educators. It was approved for in-house use by the Academic Council of the Tata Institute and recommended by the Association of Schools of Social Work in India to all the institutions for social work education in India.

The declaration is worded as a declaration and not as a code, as the former was considered the first step before the latter can be undertaken. In fact, some professional social workers were not even sure whether they would ever want a code that can be "used" by some to monitor others' work. It was considered important to qualify social workers as "professional" as India has a widely prevalent practice by voluntary and "untrained" social workers. The latter group is not homogeneous and the professional social workers, who deliberated on this declaration, had no mandate from this group to include them.

The value framework of the TISSSWEF Declaration (1997) integrates the partnership vision of people-centred development into the values listed by the International Federation of Social Workers (IFSW) and the International Association of Schools of Social Work (IASSW). They considered the following values central to the role of social workers and schools of social work: life; freedom and liberty; equality and non-discrimination; justice; solidarity; social responsibility; evolution, peace and non-violence; and relation between humankind and nature

(United Nations, 1992). These values are indigenised in the Indian context and classified based on Levy's (1973) classification of values.

Levy (1973) has classified the values of social work profession into three:

1. Preferred conceptions of people such as the belief in individual's inherent worth and dignity, capacity and drive toward constructive change, mutual responsibility, need to belong, uniqueness and common human needs.
2. Preferred outcomes for people such as the belief in society's obligation to provide opportunities for individual growth and development, to provide resources and services to help people meet their needs and to avoid such problems as hunger and to provide equal opportunities to participate in the moulding of society.
3. Preferred instrumentalities for dealing with people such as the belief that people should be treated with respect and dignity, have the right to self-determination, be encouraged to participate in social change and be recognised as unique individuals.

In December 2000, the committee of the UGC-sponsored Review of Social Work Education in India, invited feedback from all the institutions for social work education in India with reference to the following questions: Whether they are using the document in teaching history and philosophy of social work or other courses and/or in field work supervision; if they are using it, then its usefulness and need for changes in the document for further relevance. Subsequently, the Bombay Association of Trained Social Workers (BATSW) also sent the document to all its members for feedback. Their feedback was used by BATSW to revise the document in 2002.

The value framework of the Revised Declaration of Ethics for Professional Social Workers (2002) reads as follows:

"As a professional social worker, I pledge to promote the following values in myself, in the profession and in the society:

1. I pledge to perceive people as having inherent worth and dignity, irrespective of their attributes and achievements and having the capability of continuing development; and I pledge to perceive people as part of nature, needing to live in harmony with other forms of life.
2. I pledge to work towards the well-being of all people, through the achievement of the following goals:
   — Equity, non-hierarchy and non-discrimination and democratic pluralism of human groups in terms of race, nationality, colour, caste, religion, tribe, language, regional origin, gender, sexual orientation and other such factors, and condemnation of marginalisation and segregation among them.
   — Social, economic, political and legal justice, ensuring universal and equitable access to essential resources and protective safeguards for the marginalised people.
   — Basic human needs such as health, livelihood, shelter, community identity and interdependence, to be met as human rights.
   — Democracy in the systems such as family, community, state, market and media.
3. I pledge to work with people, guided by the following values:
   — Honesty, personal integrity and accountability.
   — Solidarity and partnership with the marginalised people.
   — Peace and non-violence for resolving conflicts with self, others and the environment.
   — Cooperation and collaborations, instead of competition, as the principle of interaction.

The ethical responsibilities are listed in the TISSWEF Declaration (1997) in the following areas: Self and the Profession; People in Need; The Society and the State; Co-workers and Employing Organisations; and Social Work Education and Research.

Seeking an understanding of self and change in attitudes and prejudices, which affect work, are considered the first ethical responsibility of professional social workers. Sensitivity and respect for others are considered necessary for avoiding stereotypes and recognising individuality in each person. Spirit of inquiry into relevant knowledge in the changing socio-economic, geographical and cultural context is emphasised. Caution is to be taken that knowledge, power and status as a professional are not to be used for personal gains. Besides the self, the social work profession has to be constantly reviewed to ensure its credibility and integrity.

Professional social workers' primary accountability is stressed to be with the marginalised and other people in need with whom they work. Empathy is considered necessary for giving credence/value to their life experiences. Systemic change is to be targetted at on behalf of and in partnership with them. Partnership with people should aim at facilitating mutual reflection on the life situation of both. People themselves have to play an active role in relation to the course of action to be taken about their life situation. Their access to resources and opportunities have to be facilitated.

The declaration considers promoting implementation of the Fundamental Rights and the Directive Principles enshrined in the Indian Constitution, an ethical responsibility of professional social workers. The social worker's work should promote equity, justice, non-violence, self-determination and people-centredness in the society, social systems, state policies and legislation. They need to encourage informed participation by people in shaping societal and state interventions.

Respect for inherent worth and dignity needs to be extended to all the co-workers, who include social workers, other professionals, auxiliary workers, volunteers and all those involved in the development process, within and across organisations. Personal and professional differences need to be accepted and collective reflection and democratic decision making need to be facilitated. Social workers need to periodically monitor and evaluate the organisation's policies and programmes through maintaining records, self-reflection on people's feedback and feedback from co-workers.

When teaching and training, the social worker's ethical responsibility is to be conversant with the learners' needs and knowledge. The importance of partnership between practitioners and educators needs to be recognised for the purpose of relevant education and training. Undertaking demonstration of innovative field action projects and contributing to the knowledge base of social work education, through practice, wisdom, documentation, as well as research, are an educator's ethical responsibility.

When carrying out a research, social workers should carefully select the topic for research, considering its possible consequences for human beings. The informants need to be considered as co-partners in understanding the phenomenon, by respecting their knowledge and attitude about their life situation and sharing and interpreting the findings with them.

In carrying out these diverse and sometimes conflicting responsibilities to self and the profession, the marginalised and other people in need, the society and the state, co-workers and employing organisations, and social work education and research, social workers may encounter a wide range of ethical dilemmas. The ethical dilemmas that are frequently faced in social work practice are related to confidentiality, truth-telling, paternalism and self-determination, the obligation to adhere to laws, policies and regulations, and the relationship between personal and professional values (Reamer, 1987).

Approach to Intervention

In activist social work, social workers are not saviours or liberators of the vulnerable groups, but are partners with them in the spirit of solidarity for achieving systemic change. Social work input should be such that people themselves play a dominant role for their development (Ramachandran, 1988). This may be done by the process of empowerment.

Empowerment is the process of gaining control over self, ideology and resources which determine power. The term empowerment refers to a range of activities from individual self assertion to collective resistance, protest and mobilisation that challenge basic power relations. It is a process aimed at changing the nature and direction of system forces such as the family, caste and class system, religion, top-down development models and so on, which marginalise the vulnerable groups. It does so in peaceful and non-violent approaches in the spirit of *ahimsa*. The process of empowerment should generate new notions of power. We need the power of sharing, giving, creating and developing the potential of every human being (Batliwala, 1993). An activist seeks to activate, support and honour people's ability to know their own knowing. Practice is based on people's strengths rather than problems and is value-based rather than method-based (Weick, 1994).

Challenges Ahead

The vision of the professional social workers' role, as partners with people as against the traditional role of benefactors, is full of challenges. A high status is attached to the American paradigm even in other countries, especially the developing countries. The Eurocentrism in our politics, our language and our thinking, made this a natural process. The social work profession in India still carries the legacy of the elitist urban middle class Western ethical framework which has led to more or less a hierarchical approach of work with people.

As an outcome of the Conference organised on Movements and Campaigns by and for the Marginalised Groups, Desai and Narayan (1998) identified the following tasks that social work profession has to undertake with reference to its vision for people-centred development. While making a commitment of solidarity with the marginalised groups there is a need to question the traditionally valued principles of objectivity, non-judgmental attitudes and controlled emotional involvement. The culture of confidentiality needs to be demystified. There is a need to develop an egalitarian and non-hierarchical approach in not only work with people but also with research respondents, students and co-workers. Alliances need to be formed with others who are working towards the same goals. Basically, the paradigms for professional intervention in practice, research and teaching need to be redefined.

Dealing with the legacy of professionalism of Western urban and middle class paradigm of social work, and its functionality with reference to the job market, is the major challenge that the profession in India faces in moving towards people-centred development. Desai and Narayan (1998) discuss elitism in social work, depoliticisation of social work and social action, diversity of approaches, inadequate multidisciplinary orientation, gap between practice and research and the need for humanising research, as challenges that need urgent attention.

Elitism in social work with reference to the urban middle class background of the students and the educators and the pulls of the funding organisations have to be dealt with in a planned way rather than denying it or wishing it away. The levels of education and specialisations need to be revamped. The vocabulary of the profession which has words such as 'client system' for the people and 'catalyst' to denote the role of the social worker also needs a relook. Indigenised practice is needed for relevance but in the context of globalisation. Social action has to be promoted while valuing the diversity of approaches to intervention, such as charity and clinical social work. Activism has to be promoted even in the academic field. It implies acceptance of politicisation in the profession. While acknowledging social work profession's unique contribution with reference to intervention with people's problems, the profession has to ally itself with other disciplines that are contributing to people-centred development in order for development to be people-centred rather than discipline-centred. Social change was never an exclusive domain of social work, but today all professionals need to join hands to achieve the goals of people-centred development. A people-centred approach has to be deprofessionalised. The social work profession has to bring a new rigour for relevance and credibility in this scenario. This also means integrating practice and research instead of making them independent careers. While doing that, research has to become more humanised (Desai and Narayan, 1998). These and other related issues need serious consideration at all levels.

Summary Chart 10

Historical Mode of Production and Systemic Marginalisation

	Historical Period	*Mode of Production*	*System of Marginal-isation*	*Strata*	*Justifying Ideology*
1.	Prehistoric	Hunting and gathering	—	(a) Tribal chief (b) Medicine men (c) People	Based on merits, not inherited
2.	Ancient and Medieval	Agriculture and horticulture	Marriage	(a) Husband (b) Wife	Sexism
			Slavery	(a) Owner (b) Owned	Racism
			Feudalism	(a) Lord (b) Serf	
3.	Modern	Industriali-sation	Class	(a) Capitalist (b) Labour	Liberalism Social darwinism
			Coloni-sation	(a) Coloniser (b) Colonised	Eurocentrism
			Nation-state	(a) State (b) People	Nationalism
			Develop-ment	(a) Developed (b) Under-developed	Eurocentrism
4.	Post-modern	Post-indust-ralisation	Neo-colonisation Globali-sation	(a) Global corporations (b) All others	Neo-liberalism

Summary Chart 11

Systemic Marginalisation of Vulnerable Groups

Prejudicing ideologies

↓↑

Inherent mental/physical incapacities

↓↑

Role stereotypes

↓↑

Access to resources

↓↑

Power

↓↑

Hierarchy of status

↓↑

Prejudice

↓↑

Conditional opportunities

↓↑

Discrimination

↓↑

Intolerance

↓↑

Violence

Summary Chart 12

Prejudicing Ideologies and Marginalised Groups

Constructs of Prejudice	*Prejudicing Ideology*	*Marginalised Groups*
Sex	Sexism	Women, eunuchs
Age	Ageism	Children, older persons
Abilities	Ableism	Differently-abled
Ethnicity	Ethnocentrism	Ethnic groups other than one's own
Caste	Casteism, brahminism	Dalits
Race	Racism	Non-white peoples
Class	Liberalism, classism	Poverty groups
Colonisation Development	Eurocentrism	Non-European peoples/nations

EPILOGUE

Implications for Contemporary Social Work Education

THE CONTEMPORARY CONTEXT AND OBJECTIVES OF SOCIAL WORK PROFESSION

The ex-colonies, known as the developing nations, have been pressured to privatise, liberalise and globalise, having been victims of debt trap, by the international eco-political institutions. These changes promote minimum government interference and consider market as the sole social regulator. The result of the various components of these processes has been found to be environmental devastation, tragic and unmanageable social displacement and the wiping out of cultural and biological diversity, much of it irretrievably lost, without compensation to those reliant on it. Mass media and corporate consumerist culture have been the main agents of commodification and homogenisation of cultural diversity. The domination of Western science and technology has swept away very diverse and valuable knowledge systems and technologies based on centuries of experience. This has resulted in increased unemployment, indebtedness and abject poverty.

The emerging approaches to counter globalisation are action groups inspired by the philosophy of Paulo Freire, Gandhi and others resulting in the new social movements, the second wave feminism, that have contributed to the resurgence of the civil society and multiculturalism, aiming towards sustainable and people-centred development. Social work profession, in these times, has a very significant role to play in partnership with these ideologies and groups, at the national and the international levels.

In this context, the objectives of contemporary social work profession are identified as follows:

- Promote the values of social equity, local self-governance, democratic pluralism, people's participation and peaceful coexistence.
- Critique the ideologies that lead to systemic domination and marginalisation of vulnerable groups because of their sex, ethnicity, age, health, economic background and other such attributes, leading to marginalisation of vulnerable groups such as children, youth, women, older persons, persons with varying sexual orientations, disabilities, mental or terminal illness, the labour class, Dalits, tribals/indigenous people, undertrials, institutionalised persons, victims of abuse and trafficking, dependent migrants and immigrants, displaced persons, refugees and victims of armed conflict.
- Identify the roles played by the socio-economic-political systems of family, community, state, corporate sector and mass media in society, especially in reinforcing such domination and marginalisation.

- Analyse the role played by the state, the legal and judicial systems, the welfare and development policies and schemes, influenced by international institutions.
- Work towards democratisation of the above systems, aiming at empowerment of people to meet their basic needs of food, water, livelihood and employment, health, housing, environmental sustainability, and literacy and basic education and relief and rehabilitation of victims of emergency situations such as displacements, trafficking, disasters and collective violence.
- Develop and use culture-sensitive methods of social change, such as clinical/ecological/integrated social work, management of voluntary organisations, policy and programme planning, monitoring and evaluation, social action and participation in social movements, non-formal education and participatory training and legal aid, advocacy and public interest litigations.
- Organise social work knowledge, as an integration of knowledge and action, based on a critical inquiry into practice wisdom, practice-based and participatory research, documentation of best practices, policy analysis and multidisciplinary and applied social science knowledge, in tune with the above values.
- Use social work knowledge through student-centred class room teaching and learning, self-study, field practicum and practice-based research, to educate students for developing social work personnel for social work practice, research, administration, education and training.

OBJECTIVES OF SOCIAL WORK EDUCATION

Based on the objectives of contemporary professional social work, contemporary social work education may have the following information, attitude and skill objectives, that need to be met in an integrated manner, through classroom teaching and learning, self study, field practicum and practice-based research:

Information Objectives

- Understand the dynamics of the socio-economic-political systems of family, community, state, corporate sector, mass media and international institutions.
- Analyse the role played by the state, political, legal and judicial systems, the welfare and development policies and schemes, influenced by international institutions.

Attitude Objectives

- Critique the ideologies that lead to systemic domination and marginalisation of vulnerable groups because of their sex, ethnicity, age, health, economic background and other such attributes, and develop sensitivity to children, youth, women, older persons, persons with varying sexual orientations, disabilities, mental or terminal illness, the labour class, Dalits, tribals/indigenous people, undertrials, institutionalised persons, victims of abuse and trafficking, dependent migrants and immigrants, displaced persons, refugees and victims of armed conflict.
- Promote the values of social equity, local self-governance, democratic pluralism, people's participation and peaceful coexistence.

Skill Objectives

- Obtain skills for democratisation of the socio-economic-political systems, aiming at empowerment of people to meet their basic needs of food and nutrition, water, livelihood and employment, health, housing, environmental sustainability, and literacy and basic education, and relief and rehabilitation of victims of emergency situations such as displacements, trafficking, disasters and collective violence.

- Learn methods and skills of social work management of voluntary organisations, policy and programme planning, implementation, monitoring and evaluation, social action and participation in social movements, non-formal education and participatory training and legal aid, advocacy and public interest litigations, networking and practice-based research.

Objectives by Levels of Social Work Education

Social work education is provided at the Bachelor's, Master's, M.Phil. and doctoral levels, requiring increasing order of advancement of objectives. The objective of the Bachelor's programme in social work is to prepare general practitioners for direct practice. The objective of the Master's programme in social work is to prepare general and specialised practitioners for direct practice and administration. The objective of the M.Phil. and doctoral programmes in social work is to prepare social work educators and researchers.

SUBJECT FRAMEWORK FOR SOCIAL WORK EDUCATION

Drawing from the overall objectives of social work education, the Social Work Education and Practice Cell promotes the following framework of subject modules and sub-themes:

All the social work students need to have a foundation of liberal arts subjects (humanities/social sciences) at the Bachelor's level and/or an inter-disciplinary and applied social sciences at the Master's level. They need to learn about the ideologies that historically lead to domination and marginalisation and ideologies that guide developmental social work intervention. They then need to understand the roles played by the social systems, in the society, especially in reinforcing marginalisation of vulnerable groups and deprivation of their basic needs; and the application of social work methods to change these systems. A focus on the system of state with specific reference to its development policies and programmes and their impact on basic needs and marginalisation of vulnerable groups, is necessary for social workers. The methods of social work intervention can address these dynamics, in order to have a value-based and holistic approach to the problem areas of work. Field practicum is needed to provide guided field exposure and practice of interventions in these areas. Social work students may opt to get focussed training in working for some basic needs as human rights, with reference to some marginalised/vulnerable groups, and in some emergency situations. The following are, therefore, proposed as the subject modules in social work curriculum planning:

1. Liberal Arts and/or Interdisciplinary and Applied Social Sciences
2. Ideologies for Social Change and Social Work
3. Approaches and Methods of Social Change and Social Work
4. Socio-Economic Systems and Social Work
5. Governance and Development
6. Rights to Basic Needs and Social Work
7. Marginalisation of Vulnerable Groups and Social Work
8. Victims of Emergency Situations and Social Work.
9. Social Work Field Practicum.

1. Liberal Arts and/or Interdisciplinary and Applied Social Sciences

Humanities

- English Language and Literature
- Hindi/Local Language and Literature
- Philosophy
- Fine Arts
- History

Social Sciences

- Psychology
- Sociology
- Anthropology
- Political Science
- Economics

Inter-Disciplinary and Applied Social Sciences

- Human Development
- Food and Nutrition
- Education Extension
- Applied Psychology
- Applied Sociology
- Tribal Anthropology
- Political Economy
- Demography and Population Dynamics

2. Ideologies for Social Change and Social Work

- History of Ideologies for Social Change and Social Work

- Contemporary Ideologies for Social Change and Social Work

3. Approaches and Methods of Social Change and Social Work

- Clinical Social Work
- Ecological/Integrated Social Work
- Management of Voluntary Organisations
- Policy and Programme Planning, Monitoring and Evaluation
- Social Action and Participation in Social Movements
- Non-Formal Education and Participatory Training
- Social Work Research
- Social Work in Emergency Situations
- Spirituality and Social Work

4. Socio-Economic Systems and Social Work

- Individual, Family and Social Work
- Community and Social Work
- Corporate Sector and Social Work
- Mass Media and Social Work
- Groups/Self Help Groups/Cooperatives and Social Work

5. Governance and Development

- Social Legislation, Legal System and Legal Advocacy
- Development Policies, Schemes and Administration
- The International Institutions and Globalisation
- Development Alternatives
- Municipal Administration and Urban Development

- Panchayati Raj Institutions and Rural Development
- Welfare Policies, Schemes and Administration

6. Rights to Basic Needs and Social Work

- Food and Water Security and Social Work
- Livelihood Employment and Social Work
- Environmental Sustainability and Social Work
- Land and Social Work
- Housing and Social Work
- Consumerism, Protection and Social Work
- Physical Health and Social Work
- Mental Health and Social Work
- Sexuality and Social Work
- Literacy and Basic Education and Social Work

7. Marginalisation of Vulnerable Groups and Social Work

- Children and Social Work
- Adolescents/Youth and Social Work
- Gerontological Social Work
- Women's Issues and Social Work
- Persons with Disabilities and Social Work
- Labour and Social Work
- Dalits and Social Work
- Tribals and Social Work

8. Victims of Emergency Situations and Social Work

- Displacement, Resettlement and Social Work
- Trafficking in Persons and Social Work
- Criminology and Social Work

- Substance Abuse and Social Work
- Disaster Management and Social Work
- Communalism, Collective Violence and Social Work

9. Social Work Field Practicum

- Skill Workshops for Self-Awareness and Relationships
- Organisational Visits
- Concurrent Field Placement
- Skill Workshops for Social Work Techniques
- Practice-Based Research
- Field Action Projects
- Rural Camp/Study Tour
- Social Work in Emergency Situations
- Block Placement

Sub-Themes

The sub-themes of the subjects may include the following:

- Theories, concepts and conceptual framework
- Historical and contemporary scenario
- International, national and local context
- Demographics and issues in urban/rural areas
- Structure and processes of systems involved
- Review of relevant development and welfare policies, schemes and laws
- Impact on rights to basic needs and marginalisation of vulnerable groups
- Peoples' movements and NGO initiatives
- Methods, techniques, skills and process of social work intervention

METHODOLOGY OF SOCIAL WORK EDUCATION

Methodology in social work education is as important to the learning process as methodology in social work practice is to the problem-solving process. In order for the teacher-learner transaction to give the same dynamics to training as the worker-client transaction gives to practice, the educator should be a facilitator of learning rather than merely a transmitter of knowledge. The participation model of education is, therefore, more appropriate for social work education (Hokenstad and Rigby, 1977).

In social work education, the instructor is not the pre-eminent possessor of knowledge. Learners also bring their own interpretative powers to life experiences. Both are co-sharers in the creation of what is known. When no particular interpretation deserves to have a privileged status, then the intellectual skill of critique is essential. Students must learn how to approach whatever content is presented with means for critically assessing its virtues and shortcomings. To prepare students as reflective practitioners there is a need for expanded ways for them to appreciate their own wisdom and creativity (Weick, 1994).

References

Abraham, C.E., 1993, The Rise and Growth of Christianity in India. In H. Bhattacharyya (Ed.) *The Cultural Heritage of India.* Volume IV, Calcutta: The Ramakrishna Mission, 547-570.

Agarwal, M.M., 1998, *Ethics and Spirituality.* Shimla: Indian Institute of Advanced Study.

Ahmad, I., 1998, Pluralism on Trial. In P.R. Ram (Ed.) *Secular Challenge to Communal Politics.* Mumbai: Vikas Adhyayan Kendra, 283-286.

Alba, R.D., 1992, Ethnicity. In E.F. Borgatta (Ed.) *Encyclopedia of Sociology.* Volume 4, New York: Macmillan, 575-584.

Alex, B., 2001, Dalit Movement Comes of Age. *Humanscape,* 8(8), 6-8.

Amin, S., 1996, Democracy in the Third World. In D.L. Sheth and A. Nandy (Eds.) *The Multiverse of Democracy.* New Delhi: Sage Publications, 78-99.

Association of Schools of Social Work in India, 1973, *Social Development Aspects of Social Education.* Kerala: ASSWI.

Austin, D.M., 1997, The Institutional Development of Social Work Education: The First 100 Years and Beyond. *Journal of Social Work Education*, 33(3), 599.

Banerjee, G.R., 1972, *Papers on Social Work: An Indian Perspective.* Bombay: Tata Institute of Social Sciences.

Barker, R.L., 1987, *The Social Work Dictionary.* Silver Spring, Maryland: National Association of Social Workers.

Bartlett, H., 1970, *The Common Base of Social Work Practice.* New York: National Association of Social Workers.

Batliwala, S., 1993, *Empowerment of Women in South Asia: Concepts and Practices.* Colombo: Asian-South Pacific Bureau of Adult Education.

Baxi, U., 1997, Activism at Crossroads with Signposts. In N. Bava (Ed.) *Non-Governmental Organisations in Development Theory and Practice.* New Delhi: Kanishka Publishers, 55-67.

—, 1998, The State and Human Rights Movements in India. In M. Mohanty, P.N. Mukherji and O. Tornquist (Eds.) *People's Rights: Social Movements and the State in the Third World.* New Delhi: Sage Publications, 335-352.

Belov, G., 1986, *What is the State?* Moscow: Progress Publishers.

Berbeshkina, Z., Yakovleva, L. and Zerkin, D., 1985, *What is Historical Materialism?* Moscow: Progress Publishers.

Bhaiya, A. and Menon-Sen, K., 1996, Feminist Training: Precepts and Practice: Experiences in the Mahila Samakhya Programme.

Bhargava, R., 1999, Introducing Multiculturalism. In R. Bhargava, A.K. Bagchi, & R. Sudarshan (Eds.) *Multiculturalism, Liberalism and Democracy.* New Delhi: Oxford University Press, 1-57.

Bharucha, R., 1998, Towards a Secular Cultural Movement: Critical Hypotheses, Strategies and Models. *The Indian Journal of Social Work*, 59(1), 498-512.

Bhasin, K. and Khan, N.S., 1986, *Some Questions on Feminism and its Relevance in South Asia.* New Delhi: Kali for Women.

Bhattacharyya, H., 1983, Indian Ethics. In H. Bhattacharyya (Ed.) *The Cultural Heritage of India.* Volume II, Calcutta: The Ramakrishna Mission, 620-644.

Bhowmick, S.K., 1998, The Labour Movement in India: Present Problems and Future Perspectives. *The Indian Journal of Social Work*, 59(2), 147-166.

Boguslaw, R., 1992, Liberalism/Conservatism. In E.F. Borgatta (Ed.) *Encyclopedia of Sociology*. Volume 3, New York: Macmillan, 1112-1120.

Bombyk, M. 1995, Progressive Social Work. In *Encyclopedia of Social Work*. Washington, D.C.: National Association of Social Workers, 1933-1942.

Bose, A., 1964, Philosophy in Popular Literature. In H. Bhattacharya (Ed.) *The Cultural Heritage of India*. Volume III, Calcutta: The Ramakrishna Mission, 458-470.

Brandon, D., 1976, *Zen in the Art of Helping*. London: Routledge and Kegan Paul.

Brandwein, R., 1990, Women's Issues, Women's Studies and Feminism. In F.M. Yasas and V. Mehta (Eds.) *Exploring Feminist Visions: Case Studies on Social Justice Issues*. Pune: Streevani and International Association of Schools of Social Work, 4-8.

Brieland, D., 1987, History and Evolution of Social Work Practice. In *Encyclopedia of Social Work*. Silver Spring, Maryland: National Association of Social Workers, 739-754.

Britannica.com, 2000.

Capra, F., 1982, *The Turning Point: Science, Society and Rising Culture*. London: Flaming.

—, 1996, *The Web of Life*. New York: Anchor Books.

Cleaver, H., 1993, Socialism. In W. Sachs (Ed.) *The Development Dictionary*. Johannesburg: Witwatersrand University Press.

Cox, D., 1993, Social Work Practice and Education and People-Centred Development in the Asian-Pacific Region. *The Indian Journal of Social Work*, 54(3).

Creighton, A.C., 1992, Democracy. In E.F. Borgatta (Ed.) *Encyclopedia of Sociology*. Volume 1, New York: Macmillan, 430-434.

Dasgupta, S. (Ed.), 1967, *Towards a Philosophy of Social Work in India*. Delhi: Popular Book Services.

—, 1987, Social Action. In *Encyclopaedia of Social Work in India.* Volume 3, New Delhi: Ministry of Welfare, 26-37.

Desai, A.S., 1985, The Foundations of Social Work Education in India and Some Issues. *The Indian Journal of Social Work,* 46(1), 41-57.

Desai, M., 1991, Issues Concerning the Setting Up of Social Work Specializations in India. *International Social Work,* 34(1), 83-95.

—, 1997, Literature on Social Work Profession in India 1936-1996: An Overview. *The Indian Journal of Social Work*, 58(2), 149-160.

— and Narayan, L., 1998, Challenges for Social Work Profession Towards People-Centred Development. In M. Desai, A. Monteiro and L. Narayan (Eds.) *Towards People-Centred Development.* Part 2, Mumbai: Tata Institute of Social Sciences, 531-558.

Dhanagare, D.N., 1988, Action Groups and Social Transformation in India. *Lokayan Bulletin*, 6(5), 37-59.

Dietrich, G., 2000a, Alliance of People's Movements & Critique of 'Development' -- The Indian Experience. *Vikalp/Alternatives,* 8(1&2), 127-138.

—, 2000b, Feminism in the Nineties. *Vikalp/Alternatives,* 8(1&2), 37-46.

Dominelli, L., 2002, *Feminist Social Work Theory and Practice.* New York: Palgrave.

Encyclopaedia Britannica, 2001

Feibleman, J.K., 1986, *Understanding Philosophy: A Popular History of Ideas.* New York: Souvenir Press.

Fink, H., 1981, *Social Philosophy.* London: Methuen.

Freire, P., 1972, *Pedagogy of the Oppressed.* London: Penguin Books.

Gandhi, P.K. (Ed.), 1985, *Social Action through Law: Partnership for Social Justice.* New Delhi: Concept Publishing Co.

Gardner, K. and Lewis, D., 1996, *Anthropology, Development and the Post-Modern Challenge.* London: Pluto Press.

Geiger, G.R., 1947, *Philosophy and the Social Order: An Introductory Approach.* Boston: Houghton Mifflin Co.

George, V., Ramakrishnan, A.K. and Cheriyan, G., 1997, Ecumenical Response to Globalisation. *Lokayan Bulletin,* 13(5), 61-64.

Giddens, A., 1993, *Sociology*. Oxford: Polity Press.

Giroux, H.A., 1991, Introduction to Modernism, Postmodernism, and Feminism: Rethinking the Boundaries of Educational Discourse. In H.A. Giroux (Ed.) *Post-Modernism, Feminism, and Cultural Politics: Redrawing Educational Boundaries*. Albany: State University of New York Press, 1-59.

Glossary of Terms, 1998, In P.R. Ram (Ed.) *Secular Challenge to Communal Politics*. Mumbai: Vikas Adhyayan Kendra, 295-301.

Goldstein, H., 1973, *Social Work Practice: A Unitary Approach*. Columbia, South Carolina: University of South Carolina Press.

Gordon, W.E. and Schutz, M.L., 1977, A Natural Basis for Social Work Specializations. *Social Work*, 22(5), 422-426.

Gore, M.S., 1965, *Social Work and Social Work Education*. Bombay: Asia Publishing House.

—, 1966, The Cultural Perspective in Social Work in India. *International Social Work*, 9(3), 6-16.

—, 1972, Foreword. In G.R. Banerjee (Ed.) *Papers on Social Work: An Indian Perspective*. Bombay: Tata Institute of Social Sciences, iii-iv.

—, 1987, Social Reform. In *Encyclopaedia of Social Work in India*. Volume 3, New Delhi: Ministry of Welfare, 83-93.

—, 1993, *The Social Context of an Ideology: Ambedkar's Political and Social Thought*. New Delhi: Sage Publications.

—, 1997, A Historical Perspective on the Social Work Profession. *The Indian Journal of Social Work*, 58(3), 442-455.

Graves, R.N., 1995, Atheism and Agnosticism. In *International Encyclopaedia of Sociology*. London: Ftzroy Dearborn Publishers, 101-104.

Greenwood, E., 1981, Attributes of a Profession Revisited. In N. Gilbert and H. Specht (Eds.) *The Emergence of Social Welfare and Social Work*. Itasca, Illinois: P.E. Peacock Publishers, 255-276.

Grewal, J.S., 1999, Us and Them. *Humanscape*, 6(4), 19-24.

Growth of Human Civilization, 1993, *(History) Standard IX*. Pune: Maharashtra State Board of Secondary and Higher Secondary Education.

Grusky, D.B., and Takata, A.A., 1992, Social Stratification. In E.F. Borgatta (Ed.) *Encyclopedia of Sociology*. Volume 4, New York: Macmillan, 1955-1970.

Haq, M.U., 1998, *Reflections on Human Development.* Delhi: Oxford University Press.

Hartman, A., and Laird, J., 1983, *Family-Centered Social Work Practice*. New York: The Free Press.

Heberle, R., 1968, Types and Functions of Social Movement. In *International Encyclopedia of Social Sciences*. MacMillan Press, 438-444.

History of India, 1994, *(Ancient Period) Standard VI.* Pune: Maharashtra State Bureau of Textbook Production and Curriculum Research.

----, 1995, *(Medieval Period) Standard VII.* Pune: Maharashtra State Bureau of Textbook Production and Curriculum Research.

----, 1996, *(Modern Period) Standard VIII.* Pune: Maharashtra State Bureau of Textbook Production and Curriculum Research.

Hokenstad, M.C., and Rigby, B.D., 1977, *Participation in Teaching and Learning: An Idea Book for Social Work Educators.* New York: International Association of Schools of Social Work.

Hollis, E.V. and Taylor, A.L., 1951, *Social Work Education in the United States.* New York: Columbia University Press.

Hopps, J.G. and Collins, P.M., 1995, Social Work Profession Overview. In *Encyclopedia of Social Work.* Washington, D.C.: National Association of Social Workers, 2266-2281.

— and Pinderhughes, E.B., 1987, Profession of Social Work: Contemporary Characteristics. In *Encyclopedia of Social Work.* Silver Spring, Maryland: National Association of Social Workers, 351-366.

Humanscape, 1994, 1(1), 32.

Humphreys, N.A. and Dinerman, M., 1984, Professionalizing Social Work. In M. Dinerman and L.L. Geismar (Eds.) *A Quarter Century of Social Work Education.* Silver Spring, Maryland: National Association of Social Workers, 181-216.

Hunt, I., 1978, Social Work and Ideology. In N. Timms and D. Watson (Eds.) *Philosophy in Social Work*. London: Routledge and Kegan Paul, 7-25.

Ikeda, D., 1998, Towards a New Indian Renaissance. *Humanscape,* 5(2), 31-32, 35.

Imperialism and Indian Freedom Struggle, 1998, *(History) Standard X.* Pune: Maharashtra State Board of Secondary and Higher Secondary Education.

Jain, H., 1982, Jainism: Its History, Principles and Precepts. In *The Cultural* Heritage *of India.* Volume I, Calcutta: The Ramakrishna Mission Institute of Culture, 400-413.

Johnson, L.C., 1983, *Social Work Practice: A Generalist Approach.* London: Allyn and Bacon, Inc.

Jose, G., 1998, Search for Alternatives. *Humanscape,* 5(3), 17-18.

Kamenka, E., 1978, Introduction. In E. Kamenka (Ed.) *Human Rights.* London: Edward Arnold (Publishers) Ltd, 1-12.

Kappen, S., 1994, *Tradition, Modernity, Counterculture: An Asian Perspective.* Bangalore: Visthar.

Kendall, K., 1998, *IASSW: The First Fifty Years (1928-1978) A Tribute to the Founders.* Alexandria: International Association of Schools of Social Work.

---, 2000, World-Wide Beginnings of Social Work Education. *The Indian Journal of Social Work,* 61(2), 141-156.

Khinduka, S.K., 1987, Social Work and the Human Services. In *Encyclopedia of Social Work.* Silver Spring, Maryland: National Association of Social Workers, 681-695.

Korten, D.C., 1999, When Corporations Rule the World. *Humanscape,* 6(2), 8-13.

Kothari, R., 1989, An Essay on Political Action: A Mood of Pessimism, the Politics of Perseverance. *Lokayan Bulletin,* 7(4), 5-15.

Kundra, D.N., 1997, *A Combined Textbook of History and Civics.* New Delhi: Goyal Brothers Prakashan.

Laird, J., 1994, Introduction. In J. Laird (Ed.) *Revisioning Social Work Education: A Social Constructionist Approach.* New York: The Haworth Press Inc, 1-10.

Leiby, J., 1987, History of Social Welfare. In *Encyclopedia of Social Work.* Silver Spring, Maryland: National Association of Social Workers, 755-777.

Levy, C.S., 1973, The Value Base of Social Work. *Journal of Education for Social Work,* 9(1), 34-42.

Lobo, G.V., 1991, *Human Rights in Indian Situation*. New Delhi: Commission for Justice, Peace and Development.

Macarov, D., 1995, *Social Welfare: Structure and Practice.* London: Sage Publications.

Mahadevan, T.M.P., 1982, The Religio-Philosophic Culture of India. In *The Cultural Heritage of India.* Volume I, Calcutta: The Ramakrishna Mission Institute of Culture, 163-181.

Manshardt, M.C., 1967, *Pioneering on Social Frontiers in India.* Bombay: Lalvani Publishing House.

Marshall, G. (Ed.), 1994, *The Concise Oxford Dictionary of Sociology.* New York: Oxford University Press.

Mathew, G., 1987, Casework. In *Encyclopaedia of Social Work in India.* Volume 1, New Delhi: Ministry of Welfare, 59-66.

McCasland, S.V., Cairns, G.E. and Yu, D.C., 1969, *Religions of the World.* New York: Random House.

Menon, M., 1995, The Green Army. *Humanscape,* 3(2), 30-31.

Merton, R.K., 1960, *Some Thoughts on the Professions in American Society.* Brown University.

Minogue, K.R., 1978, Natural Rights, Ideology and the Game of Life. In E. Kamenka (Ed.) *Human Rights.* London: Edward Arnold (Publishers) Ltd, 13-35.

Mohanty, M., 1998, Introduction: Towards a Creative Theory of Social Transformation. In M. Mohanty, P.N. Mukherji and O. Tornquist (Eds.) *People's Rights: Social Movements and the State in the Third World.* New Delhi: Sage Publications, 9-28.

Monteiro, A. and Lingam, L., 1998, Towards a Common Voice?: An Introduction to Movements and Campaigns in India. *The Indian Journal of Social Work,* 59(1), 3-34.

Morehouse,W. and Grossman, R., 1999, The Rights of Capital Above the Rights of Humans. *Humanscape,* 6(7), 6-7.

Mukherji, R., 1983, The Philosophy of Mysticism. In H. Bhattacharya (Ed.) *The Cultural Heritage of India.* Volume III, Calcutta: The Ramakrishna Mission, 449-457.

Muricken, A., 1998, Foreword. In P.R. Ram (Ed.) *Secular Challenge to Communal Politics*. Mumbai: Vikas Adhyayan Kendra, I-IX.

Muzaffar, C., 1994, *Human Rights and the New World Order*. Penang: Just World Trust.

Nagpaul, H., 1988, The Profession of Social Work in Contemporary India. *Indian Journal of Social Research*, 39(4), 339-355.

Nanavatty, M.C., 1997, Professional Associations of Social Work: An Analysis of Literature. *The Indian Journal of Social Work*, 58(2), 287-300.

Nandy, A., 1994, *The Illegitimacy of Nationalism: Rabindranath Tagore and the Politics of Self*. Delhi: Oxford University Press.

—, 1998, *The Intimate Enemy: Loss and Recovery of Self under Colonialism*. Delhi: Oxford University Press.

Nicholson, 1990, Introduction. In L.J. Nicholson (Ed.) *Feminism/ Postmodernism*. New York: Routledge.

Omvedt, G., 1994, *Dalits and the Democratic Revolution*. New Delhi: Sage Publications.

----, 1996, *Dalit Visions*. Hyderabad: Orient Longman, Tracts for the Times/8.

—, 1998, Peasants, Dalits and Women: Democracy and India's New Social Movements. In M. Mohanty, P.N. Mukherji and O. Tornquist (Eds.) *People's Rights: Social Movements and the State in the Third World*. New Delhi: Sage Publications, 223-242.

O'Rand, A.M., 1992, Social Inequality. In E.F. Borgatta (Ed.) *Encyclopedia of Sociology*. Volume 4, New York: Macmillan, 1850-1856.

Pandhe, S., 1989, *Women's Subordination (Its Origins)*. New Delhi: Kanak Publications.

Panikkar, K.N., 1995, *Culture, Ideology, Hegemony: Intellectual and Social Consciousness in Colonial India*. New Delhi: Tulika.

—, 1998, What is Communalism Today? In P.R. Ram (Ed.) *Secular Challenge to Communal Politics: A Reader*. Bombay: Vikas Adhyayan Kendra, 41-57.

Pardeck, J.T., 1996, An Ecological Approach for Social Work Intervention. *Family Therapy*, 23(3), 190-198.

Parsons, R.J., Jorgensen, J.D. and Hernandez, S.H., 1994, *The Integration of Social Work Practice.* Belmont, California: Brooks /Cole Publishing Company.

Payne, M., 2000, Social Work Theory. In M. Davies (Ed.) *The Blackwell Encyclopaedia of Social Work.* Oxford: Blackwell Publishers.

Pendse, S., 1994, Introduction. In S. Pendse (Ed.) *At Cross-Roads: Dalit Movement Today.* Bombay: Vikas Adhyayan Kendra, vii-xiii.

People's Global Action, 1998, *Lokayan Bulletin*, 14(5), 41-64.

Percival, F. and Ellington, H., 1984, *A Handbook of Educational Technology.* New York: Kogan Page.

Pereira, W., 1997, *Inhuman Rights: The Western System and Global Human Rights Abuse.* Mapusa, Goa: The Other India Press.

Pincus, A., and Minahan, A., 1973, *Social Work Practice: Model and Methods.* Itasca, Illinois: F.E. Peacock Publishers, Inc.

Pinderhughes, E., 1995, Direct Practice Overview. In *Encyclopedia of Social Work.* Washington, D.C.: National Association of Social Workers, 740-751.

Poonacha, V., 1995, *Gender within the Human Rights Discourse.* Bombay: Research Centre for Women's Studies, SNDT University.

Prabhu, P., 1998, Tribal Movements: Resistance to Resurgence. *The Indian Journal of Social Work*, 59(1), 230-255.

Puledda, S., 1998, The Essence of Humanism. *Humanscape*, 5(4), 31-32, 34.

Ram, P.R., 1998, Introduction. In P.R. Ram (Ed.) *Secular Challenge to Communal Politics: A Reader.* Mumbai: Vikas Adhyayan Kendra, I-XVII.

—, 1999, Perversion of Gandhian and National Values: The Anti-Gandhi Myths of Hindutva – 1. *Facts against Myths*, 5(1).

Ramachandran, P., 1988, *Perspective for Social Work Training: 2000 A.D.* Bombay: Tata Institute of Social Sciences (Mimeograph).

Ramaiah, A., 1998, The Plight of Dalits: A Challenge to Social Work Profession. *The Indian Journal of Social Work*, 59(1).

Ramsay, R.F., 1999, Toward a Common Paradigmatic Home: Social Work in the 21st Century. *The Indian Journal of Social Work*, 60(1), 69-86.

Random House, 1992, *Random House Webster's Unabridged Dictionary*. New York: Random House.

Rao, M., 1994, An Imagined Reality: Malthusianism, Neo-Malthusians and Population Myth. *Economic and Political Weekly*, FE40-PE41.

Rao, V.V., 1997, People's Movements: The Role of a Writer. *Lokayan Bulletin*, 13(6), 1-18.

Reader's Digest Oxford, 1993, *Word Finder*. Oxford: Clarendon Press.

Reamer, F.G., 1987, Values and Ethics. In *Encyclopedia of Social Work*. Silver Spring, Maryland National Association of Social Workers, 801-809.

—, 2001, *Ethics Education in Social Work*. Alexandria, Virginia: Council on Social Work Education.

Reid, P.N., 1995, Social Welfare History. In *Encyclopedia of Social Work*. Washington, D.C.: National Association of Social Workers Press, 2206-2225.

Ripple, L. (Ed.), 1969, *Innovations in Teaching Social Work Practice*. New York: Council for Social Work Education.

Roberts, P., 1990, *Lessons from the Past: Issues for Social Work Theory*. London and New York: Routledge.

Roche, S.E., Dewees, M., Trailweaver, R., Alexander, S., Cuddy, C. and Handy, M., 1999, *Contesting Boundaries in Social Work Education: A Liberatory Approach to Cooperative learning and Teaching*. Alexandria: Council on Social Work Education.

Rosenau, P.M., 1992, *Post-modernism and the Social Sciences: Insights, Inroads and Intrusions*. Princeton, New Jersey: Princeton University Press.

Roy, A., 1997, Civil Society and the Nation-State – In the Context of Globalisation. In A. Muricken (Ed.) *Globalisation and SAP: Trends and Impact: An Overview*. Mumbai: Vikas Adhyayan Kendra, 45-64.

Saldanha, D., 1995, State, Society and Voluntary Intervention: Reflections of Some Action Groups. In M. Savur and I. Munshi (Eds.) *Contradictions in Indian Society*. Jaipur: Rawat Publications, 189-209.

Samuel, J., 1998, Who's Afraid of NGOs?. *Humanscape*, 5(10), 34-35.

—, 1999, Only Those Have Received Who Have Given. *Humanscape,* 6(3), 6-8.

Sanghvi, S., 1982, Some Fundamental Principles of Jainism. In *The Cultural Heritage of India.* Volume I, Calcutta: The Ramakrishna Mission Institute of Culture, 434-441.

Sarkar, S., 1997, *Writing Social History.* Delhi: Oxford University Press.

Schaull, R., 1972, Foreword. In P. Freire (Ed.) *Pedagogy of the Oppressed.* London: Penguin Books, 9--14.

Sen, K., 1993, The Medieval Mystics of North India. In H. Bhattacharya (Ed.) *The Cultural Heritage of India.* Volume IV, Calcutta: The Ramakrishna Mission, 377-394.

Sen, S., 1998, Religion, Relief, Rehabilitation. *Humanscape,* 5(5), 27-30, 33.

Sethi, H., 1989, Politics, Elections and Parties: Choices Before Voluntary Groups. *Lokayan Bulletin*, 7(4), 17-23.

—, 1998, Micro-Struggles, NGO's and the State. In M. Mohanty, P.N. Mukherji and O. Tornquist (Eds.) *People's Rights: Social Movements and the State in the Third World.* New Delhi: Sage Publications, 405-420.

Shah, I., 1964, *The Sufis.* New York: Doubleday and Co., Inc.

Shankardass, V.S.T., 1997, Rules of Law, Democracy and Human Rights in India. In A. Muricken (Ed.) *Globalisation and SAP Trends and Impact: An Overview*. Mumbai: Vikas Adhyayan Kendra, 110-118.

Sharma, B.D., 1998, The People Versus the System. In M. Desai, A. Monteiro and L. Narayan (Eds.) *Towards People-Centred Development*, Mumbai: Tata Institute of Social Sciences, 44-61.

Sharma, I.C., 1980, Human Rights and Comprehensive Humanism. In A.S. Rosenbaum (Ed.) *The Philosophy of Human Rights: International Perspective.* Westport, Connecticut: Greenwood Press.

Sheafor, B.W., Horejsi, C.R. and Horejsi, G.A., 1997, *Techniques and Guidelines for Social Work Practice.* Boston: Allyn and Bacon.

Shiva, V., 1997a, The Alternative to Corporate Protectionism. *Lokayan Bulletin*, 14 (2), 31-43.

—, 1997b, Democracy in the Age of Globalisation. In A. Muricken (Ed.) *Globalisation and SAP Trends and Impact: An Overview*. Mumbai: Vikas Adhyayan Kendra, 65-78.

Siddiqui, H.Y. (Ed.), 1984, *Social Work and Social Action*. New Delhi: Harnam Publications.

—, 1997, Analysis of Literature on Social Action. *The Indian Journal of Social Work*, 58(2), 212-232.

Singhal, D.P., 1983, *A History of the Indian People*. London: Methuen.

Siporin, M., 1984, A Future for Social Work Education. In M. Dinerman and L.L. Geismar (Eds.) *A Quarter Century of Social Work Education*. National Association of Social Workers, 237-252.

Sircar, M., 1982, Mystical Approach in the Upanishads. In *The Cultural Heritage of India*. Volume I, Calcutta: The Ramakrishna Mission Institute of Culture, 366-374.

Srinivasan, A., 1994, Women and Reform of Indian Tradition: Gandhian Alternative to Liberalism. In L. Kasturi and V. Mazumdar (Eds.) *Women and Indian Nationalism*. New Delhi: Vikas Publishing House, 1-15.

Swami Ghanananda, 1987, *Sri Ramakrishna and his Unique Message*. Calcutta: Advaita Ashrama.

Swami Nirvedanada, 1993, Sri Ramakrishna and Spiritual Renaissance. In H. Bhattacharyya (Ed.) *The Cultural Heritage of India*. Volume IV, Calcutta: The Ramakrishna Mission, 653-730.

Swatija and Chayanika, 1992, *Not Just a Matter of Faith: Essays on Communalism*. Bombay: An Akshara Publication.

Swensen, C.R., 1995, Clinical Social Work. In *Encyclopedia of Social Work*. Washington, D.C.: National Association of Social Workers, 502-513.

Szelenyi, S., 1992, Socialism. In E.F. Borgatta (Ed.) *Encyclopedia of Sociology*. Volume 4, New York: Macmillan, 1858-1863.

Taraporewala, I.J.S., 1993, Zoroastrianism. In H. Bhattacharyya (Ed.) *The Cultural Heritage of India*. Volume IV, Calcutta: The Ramakrishna Mission, 533-546.

Tata Institute of Social Sciences, 1997, Towards People-centred Development: Report of TISS Diamond Jubilee Conference. Mumbai.

Tata Institute of Social Sciences Social Work Educators Forum (TISSSWEF), 1997, Declaration of Ethics for Professional Social Workers. *The Indian Journal of Social Work*, 58(2), 335-341.

Teltumbde, A., 1998, Theorising Dalit Movement: A Viewpoint. *Alternatives*, 6(2), 25-40.

---, 2000, Theorising the Dalit Movement: A Viewpoint. *Vikalp/Alternative*, 8(1&2), 71-92.

Thapar, R., 1998, Communalism and the Historical Legacy: Some Facts. In P.R. Ram (Ed.) *Secular Challenge to Communal Politics.* Mumbai: Vikas Adhyayan Kendra, 6-24.

The World Book Encyclopedia, 1988, Chicago: The World Book, Inc.

Tourse, R.W.C., 1995, Special-Interest Professional Associations. In *Encyclopedia of Social Work.* Washington, D.C.: National Association of Social Workers, 2314-2320.

University Grants Commission, 1965, *Social Work Education in Indian Universities.* New Delhi.

---, 1980, *Review of Social Work Education in India: Retrospect and Prospect.* New Delhi.

---, 1990, *Report of the Curriculum Development Centre in Social Work Education.* New Delhi.

United Nations, 1992, *Human Rights: Teaching and Learning About Human Rights.* New York.

Vanina, E., 1996, *Ideas and Society in India from the Sixteenth to the Eighteenth Centuries.* Delhi: Oxford University Press.

Vas, G., 1997, *The Story of India for Children.* Noida: Blossom Books.

Voluntary Action Network India (VANI), No date, *Non-Governmental Organisations: Guidelines for Good Policy and Practice.* London: The Commonwealth Foundation.

Wagner, A., 1984, Decentralization Privatization and Deprofessionalization. Is Small Always Beautiful ? In C. Guzzetta, A.J. Katz and R.A. English (Eds.) *Education for Social Work*

Practice. Vienna: International Association of Schools of Social Work, 9-18.

Walz, T. and Ritchie, 2000, Gandhian Principles in Social Work Practice: Ethics Revisited. *Social Work,* 45(3), 213-222.

Weber, M., 1958, *The Protestant Ethic and the Spirit of Capitalism.* New York: Charles Scribner's Sons.

Weick, A., 1994, Reconstructing Social Work Education. In J. Laird (Ed.) *Revisioning Social Work Education: A Social Reconstructionist Approach.* New York: The Haworth Press, 11-30.

World History, 1996, London: Dorling Kindersley.

Yasas, F.M., 1964, *Gandhian Values and Professional Social Work Values with Special Emphasis on the Dignity of Man.* Michigan: University of Microfilms.

Zaehner, R.C., 1959, Introduction. In R.C. Zaehner (Ed.) *The Concise Encyclopaedia of Living Faiths.* Boston: Beacon Press, 15-22.

Zaehner, R.C., 1994, *Hindu and Muslim Mysticism.* Oxford: One World Publications.

Zwi Werblowsky, R.J., 1959, Judaism, or the Religion of Israel. In R.C. Zaehner (Ed.) *The Concise Encyclopedia of Living Faiths.* Boston: Beacon Press, 23-50.

Index

ableism, 180
Abraham, C.E., 116, 117
action groups
  ideologies of, 165-68
ageism, 187-88
agnosticism, 24
Agarwal, M.M., 111, 157
ahimsa
  Gandhian ideology of, 124
Ahmad, I., 162
Alba, R.D., 157
Alex, B., 171
Alexander, S., 27
Ambedkar, Babasaheb, 122
Amin, S., 170
anekantvada (non-absolutism), 109
Arya Samaj, 119
ashrama (life stages) system, 107
atheism, 24
atman (soul), 106
Austin, D.M., 79, 81

Banerjee, G.R., 138
Barker, R.L., 54, 82, 87, 88, 92, 94, 184, 185
Bartlett, H., 84, 98
Batliwala, S., 189, 196
Baxi, U., 129, 132, 172
Belov, G., 21, 61
Berbeshkina, Z., 19, 20
Berlin Wall
  falling of, 152
Bhaiya, A., 160

Bhakti movement, 24
Bhakti traditions, 114
Bhargava, R., 162, 163, 164
Bharucha, R., 171
Bhasin, K., 159
Bhattacharyya, H., 107
Bhave, Vinoba, 125
Bhoodan, 125
Bhowmick, S.K., 170
Boguslaw, R., 55, 59, 62
Bombyk, M., 184
Bose, A., 113
bourgeois revolution, 58
Brahman, 106
Brahminism, 107-8
Brahmo Samaj, 119
Brandon, D., 183
Brandwein, R., 160
Brieland, D., 77, 78
Britannica.com, 18, 63, 65
Buddhism, 23, 109-10

Cairns, G.E., 48
Capra, F., 53, 154, 159, 161, 164, 190
casteism, 188
charitable work, 76
Cheriyan, G., 153
Christ, Jesus, 46, 48
Christianity, 23, 46-47, 48, 49
  in India, 116-17
civil society
  resurgence of the, 160-62
classism, 189
Cleaver, H., 68
clinical social work, 80-83
Collins, P.M., 97
communist parties, 67
contemporary ideologies
  for social change, 151-79
  of social work profession, 180-201
Cox, D., 165
Creighton, A.C., 60, 61
Cuddy, C., 27

Dalit movement, 121-23, 128
Dalits, 121, 171
dana, 107
Dasgupta, S., 139, 140
democracy, 57, 60, 163
  types of, 60
Desai, M., 144, 147, 148, 197, 198
Dewees, M., 27
Dhanagare, D.N., 168, 174
dharma, 107
Dietrich, G., 152, 169, 170
Dinerman, M., 81, 83, 91, 92
Directive Principles of State Policy, 130-31
Dominelli, L., 101, 185

eastern religions, 23
ecological social work, 83-87
Ellington, H., 36
Encyclopaedia Britannica, 18, 67, 126
Enlightenment, 53
ethnocentrism, 188
eurocentrism, 189

Feibleman, J.K., 14, 26, 45, 46, 52
feminism, 158-60
  schools of, 158-59
feminist social work, 184-85
feudalism, 20, 47
Fink, H., 61, 67
First World, 152
French Revolution, 58, 65
Freire, Pauls, 166, 167, 168
fundamental duties, 131-32
fundamental rights, 129-30

Gandhi, Mahatma, 138
Gandhi, P.K., 140
Gandhian ideology, 24, 123-25
  and Sarvodaya movement, 125-26
Gardener, K., 64
Geiger, G.R., 54, 60
George, V., 153, 155
Giddens, A., 60
Giroux, H.A., 157
globalisation, 21, 153, 182
  components of, 153
Gokhale, Gopal Krishna, 135
Goldstein, H., 26, 27, 84
Gore, M.S., 22, 24, 66, 100, 107, 108, 118, 119, 120, 124, 125, 136, 137, 138
Graves, R.N., 24
Great Depressions
  of the 1930s, 57
Greek ideologies
  for social change, 45-46
Greenwood, E., 92
Grewal, J.S., 117, 120
Grossman, R., 155
Growth of Human Civilization, 21, 47, 49, 50
Grusky, D.B., 19, 20, 68, 157, 158

Handy, M., 27
Haq, M.U., 164
Hartman, A., 84, 85, 86
Heberle, R., 24
Hernandez, S.H., 82
Hindu reform movements, 117-21
Hinduism, 117
historical materialism
  Marxist theory of, 19, 181
History of India, 108, 118, 123
history, 18
  division of, 19
Hokenstad, M.C., 35, 212
Hollis, E.W., 98
homogenisation, 162
Hopps, J.G., 80, 97
Horejsi, C.R., 87
Horejsi, G.A., 87
human rights
  ideology of, 69-73
human rights discourse
  in India, 171
human rights movements, 172
Humphreys, N.A., 81, 83, 91, 92
Hunt, I., 14, 22

ideology(ies) 22
  and social movements, 24
  for social change, 22-24,
    classification of, 43
  of social work students, 26-27
Ikeda, D., 51, 66
Imperialism and Indian Freedom Struggle, 69, 124
Indian Constitution, 128, 171
  ideology of the, 128-32
Indian ideologies
  for social change, 104-34:
    ancient, 105-11; medieval, 111-16; modern, 116-33; implications of, 134
  of social work profession, 135-49; influences on, 150
Industrial Revolution
  in the west, 21, 182
intellectual property rights, 155
Islam, 23
  in India, 112-13
  principles of, 112

Jain, H., 108
Jainism, 23, 108-9
jati (caste) system, 107
Johnson, L.C., 90, 91
Jorgensen, J.D., 82
Jose, G., 169
Judaism, 23, 46, 48, 49
Judeo-Christian ideologies
  for social change, 46-53, 70
Judeo-Christian religions, 23

Kabir, 114
Kamenka, E., 69, 70
Kappen, S., 21, 61, 64, 181
karma, 106
Kendall, Katherine, 18, 79
Khan, N.S., 159
Khinduka, S.K., 91, 93, 99, 100, 101
knowledge-as-action, 27
Koran, 112
Korten, D.C., 153
Kothari, R., 175
Kundra, D.N., 20, 110, 112

Laird, J., 84, 85, 86, 185
Leiby, J., 55, 56, 76, 77, 79, 80
Levy, C.S., 192
Lewis, D., 64
liberalism, 57-61, 182
license *raj*, 154
Lingam, L., 170
Lobo, G.V., 72

Macarov, D., 52, 55, 57, 59, 63, 65, 77
Mahadevan, T.M.P., 106
Manshardt, M.C., 136
marginalisation
  systems of, 190
marginalised groups
  prejudicing ideologies and, 201
marriage, 20
Marshall, G., 46, 48, 49, 61, 66, 112, 158, 187, 188, 190
Marx, Karl, 66, 67

Marxism, 67
Mathew, G., 82
Mc Casland, S.V., 48, 49
Menon, M., 173
Menon-Sen, K., 160
Merton, R.K., 25
Minahan, A., 84, 93
Minogue, K.R., 72
modernism
  vs postmodernism, 177
Mohanty, M., 172
moksha, 106
Monteiro, A., 170
Morehouse, W., 155
Mukherji, R., 106
multiculturalism, 162-64
Muricken, A., 51
Muzaffar, C., 172
mysticism, 113
  of Bhakti and Sufi
    movements, 113-15

Nagpaul, H., 137
Nanavatty, M.C., 141
Nandy, A., 127, 154
Narayan, L., 197, 198
National Alliance of People's
  Movement (NAPM), 172
nationalism, 126-28
nation-states, 21, 58
neo-liberalism, 152-56, 176, 182
new social movements (NSMs),
  168-70
  in India, 170
  types of, 170-73
Nicholson, 156
non-government organisations
  (NGOs)
  ideologies of, 173-75

O'Rand, A.M., 158
Omvedt, G., 122, 123, 128, 168,
  169, 170

Pandhe, S., 20
Panikkar, K.N., 117, 127
Pardeck, J.T., 85
Parsons, R.J., 82, 84, 85, 87
patent *raj*, 154
paternity, 20
Payne, M., 77, 184
People's Global Action, 155, 161
people-centered development,
  165
Percival, F., 36
Pereira, W., 64
philanthropy, 76
philosophy, 22
  branches of, 22
Pincus, A., 84, 93
Pinderhughes, E.B., 80, 84
Plato, 65
Poonacha, V., 159
postmodernism, 156-57
  and social work, 185-86
Prabhu, P., 171
prejudicing ideologies, 187
professional attributes
  classification of, 92-93
  concept of, 91-92

professional social work
  limitations of, 182-83
progressive social work, 184
Protestantism, 51-53, 181
Puledda, S., 50

racism, 188
radical social work, 184
Ram, P.R., 21, 126, 128, 181
Ram, P.R., 58
Ramachandran, P., 196
Ramaiah, A., 122, 171
Ramakrishna Mission, 119
Ramakrishnan, A.K., 153
Ramsay, R.F., 54, 64
Random House, 90
Rao, M., 55, 56, 61
rationalism, 53-54
Readers' Digest Oxford, 187, 188
Reamer, F.G., 79, 81, 83, 94, 96, 196
Reid, P.N., 55
religion(s)
  of the world, 23
religious ideologies, 23
Renaissance movement
  in Europe, 50
resources
  and power, 189
Richmond, Mary, 79, 80
Rigby, B.D., 35, 212
Ripple, L., 25
Roberts, P., 87
Roche, S.E., 27, 185
Roman Catholic Church, 49, 52
Rosenau, P.M., 156
Roy, A., 160
Roy, Raja Ram Mohan, 118, 119
Russian Revolution, 67

Saldhana, D., 152, 165
samsara, 106
Samuel, J., 49, 174, 175
Sanghvi, S., 109
Saraswati, Dayanand, 119
Sarkar, S., 69
Sarvodaya
  Gandhian vision of, 125
Sarvodaya movement, 24, 125
satyagraha
  Gandhian ideology of, 124
Schaull, R., 165, 166
scientific charity, 76-79
scientific humanism, 54
Second World, 152
secular humanism, 50-51, 181
secular ideologies, 24
Sen, S., 113, 126, 165
Sethi, H., 125, 132, 175
sexism, 187
Shah, I., 114
Shankardass, V.S.T., 72
Sharia, 112
Sharma, B.D., 21, 60, 62, 67, 70, 152, 154, 156
Sharma, I.C., 51, 54
Sheafor, B.W., 87
Shiva, V., 154, 161
Siddiqui, H.Y., 139, 140
Sikhism, 23, 115-16

Singhal, D.P., 107, 112, 116, 119
Siporin, M., 98
Sircar, M., 110
slavery, 20
social change, 18
  history of, 18-22
  ideologies for, 22-24; western, 44-73; Indian, 104-34; contemporary, 151-79
Social Darwinism, 62-65, 182
social welfare, 79
social work education
  in India, beginning of, 135-36
  methodology of, 212
  objectives of, 204-6
social work education, 27
  beginning of, 79
  methodology of, 35-42
  modules of, 28-31
  objectives of, 27-28
  structure and content of, 31-35
social work practice, 17, 82
  levels of, 87-88
  roles of, 88-90
  types of, 87
social work profession, 25
  ideologies of: western, 75-102; Indian, 135-50; contemporary, 180-201
  objectives of, 203-4
social work, 18, 79, 137
  as a problem-solving process, 90-91
  ideologies of, 18
  professionalisation of: in western countries, 93-102; in India, 137-49
social workers, 79
  roles of, 88-90
socialism, 65-69
spirituality, 110
Srinivasan, A., 160, 161
Sufi movement, 24
Sufism, 114
sustainable development, 164
Swami Ghananandа, 23
Swami Nirvedananda, 117, 119, 120
Swensen, C.R., 82, 83
Szelenyi, S., 66, 68

Tagore, R.N., 126, 127
Takata, A.A., 19, 20, 68, 157, 158
Taraporewala, I.J.S., 111
Taylor, A.L., 98
Teltumbde, A., 121, 123, 128, 170
Thapar, R., 120
The World Book Encyclopedia, 19, 20, 22, 46, 47,49, 50, 52, 53, 57, 59, 60, 61, 65, 67, 109
Theosophical Society, 119
Third World, 152
TISS, 183
Tourse, R.W.C., 95
Trailweaver, R., 27
transnational corporations (TNCs), 154
tribal system, 19
Trinity
  doctrine of, 48

UGC, 142, 146
United Nations Declaration of
  Human Rights, 1948, 71, 129
United Nations, 58, 70, 71, 72,
  192
untouchables, 107, 121
upanishads, 106, 110
utilitarianism, 62, 64, 182

Vania, E., 114, 115
varna (colour) system, 107
Vas, G., 112, 113, 115, 116
Vedas, 105, 108
Vedic ideology, 105-8
Vedic religion, 23
Vivekanand, Swami, 119
voluntary organisations
  ideology of, 132-33
vulnerable groups
  systemic marginalisation of,
    200

Wagner, A., 100
Walz, T., 94, 124, 156
Weber, M., 52, 53
Weick, A., 35, 99, 196, 212
Western ideologies
  for social change, 44-74:
    ancient, 45-46; medieval,
    46-53; modern, 53-73;
    implications of, 74
  of social work profession,
    75-102
World capitalist system, 65
World History, 52, 58

Yakovleva, L., 19
Yoga, 106
  forms of, 106
Yu, D.C., 48

Zaehner, R.C., 23, 105, 114
Zerkin, D., 19
Zoroastrianism, 23
  in India, 111
Zwi Werblowsky, R.J., 48